An Agency Life

A MEMOIR

Scott Janzen

ISBN: 978-1-66781-676-0

Contents

Foreword

I'VE ALWAYS FELT THAT one measure of a person's popularity is in how many nicknames they have and how institutionalized those names become with others. Willie Mays was the "Say Hey Kid." Marshawn Lynch was "Beast Mode." Muhammed Ali was "The Greatest of All Time."

By this measure, then, Scott Janzen arguably goes down in the annals of Seattle agency history as one of the most popular, recognizable figures of the past few decades.

When our paths first crossed back in Seattle's halcyon days in the advertising and PR agency business in the 80s, he was simply this brash, slightly inappropriate guy named Scott. By the time our professional careers diverged 20 years later, he was known by me and many others as "Janbo" (for his Rambo-like approach to promotional marketing); "Jahms" (a derivative of Janbo if you were in a hurry and didn't want to use two syllables); "Jambalaya" (if you were feeling sufficiently Creole); "Chemo" (homage to a strange chemical his stylist applied to his hair one year to make it look more curly); and "Starving Dog" (a nod to his approach when trying to talk to pretty much any woman in a crowded bar).

He took all these names in stride, though. I think a big part of him loved that he had so many monikers, and still does to this day.

In addition to popularity, he was and is, quite simply, one of the most creative PR minds I have ever had the pleasure of working with. This is the guy, after all, who created the World's First Edible Chair as a stunt to drive traffic to the Science Center back in the day. Forget for a moment that you might be sitting on a week-old piece of salami or some Junior Mints—it generated—wait for it—worldwide press attention. Scott was also the creator of something called the Eddie Bauer Mississippi River Challenge—a two-person journey in a canoe from the headwaters of the Mississippi

River in northern Minnesota down to the delta near New Orleans. I think the Challenge was mainly an excuse for Scott to create a junket for himself so he could visit honky-tonks in a part of the country he had never been to before—but it worked. There were many other promotions and stunts Scott dreamed up where a linear thinker like me would just shake his head and say, *how the hell did he think of that one?*

At a personal level, Scott applied his creativity to helping build both our personal brands when we were in our late-20s. The vehicle was something called "Bop til Ya Drop"—a raucous boat cruise on Seattle's Elliott Bay for 125 of our friends and anyone else who wanted to shell out $20 for a four-hour descent into debauchery. Scott and I organized the whole thing and celebrated our "host-ness" by wearing tuxedos to the event. We sold out every year, always making sure we had an acceptable ratio of women to men (that is to say, more women than men) and generally had to be hand-carted off the boat at the end of the evening. Good times indeed.

Scott was also a fixture in the RAT League Softball season every summer. This was a league made up of, as the acronym would imply, people who worked in Radio, Advertising, and Television industries in Seattle. While he may not have been the quintessential five-tool player, he more than made up with it with his catcalling from the dugout and his overall intensity. If you didn't know, you'd think he was calling for a double-steal with two on and two out in the bottom of the ninth in game seven of the World Series. Similarly, in pick-up basketball games, he'd be the guy calling out defensive alignments and offensive rotations when all anyone else wanted to do was chuck balls from 25 feet. *Huh what?*

Mostly though, Scott's just a good dude. Always there for his friends. Always with a laugh or a joke, sometimes appropriate—oftentimes not. I hope the stories contained in the chapters of *An Agency Life* give the reader just a slice of the guy I've known for a good chunk of my personal and professional life. They've certainly brought back some great memories for me.

Tom Phillips/July 2021

Introduction

I'M A LUCKY DUDE.

I've spent more than 40 years in a profession I had no intention of being a part of. I was going to be a journalist, damn it—specifically, a sportswriter. My version of the old expression, tailored for the sports world: those who can, compete; those who can't, write about it.

I was a writer and editor in high school, in college, and with my hometown weekly newspaper. And since the Mariners were not going to draft me out of Seattle University to play third base, I chose to be a writer. The baseball scouts said I was "no hit, no field, and no way in hell."

When I saw an opening with the Seattle Sounders for a PR intern, I thought: as a writer, I will be working with these PR clowns forever; why not be one for a summer to see what it's all about?

The truth is, I enjoyed my time interning with the Sounders. We went to Soccer Bowl, our league's championship, over the summer. I got to go to all of our matches, and they fed me dinner at the Kingdome. Listen, as an unpaid intern, that was a big deal.

This journalism thing can wait, I reasoned. Oh well. Based on what's happened since in the world of print journalism, it seems I made the right call.

When I discovered agency public relations, my choice became even clearer. I was always a pretty creative guy, and clients loved my ideas, especially in the worlds of retail and travel.

So why a book? And why now?

Well, I'm still young enough to remember these stories. I wanted to get them down on paper somewhere before they all went away. And as every year goes by, I'm losing many of my heroes in the PR and advertising world—either to death or retirement. Some would argue that's the same thing, but that's a discussion for another time.

This book is written in three parts:

The early years: growing up and driving my sisters and neighbors insane; my first two pre-agency jobs.

The agency years: working with brilliant colleagues at brilliant agencies like Elgin Syferd, BPN, WONGDOODY, DDB Seattle and The Fearey Group.

The entrepreneur years: opening my own firm, Janzen & Associates, in its various forms; going to the client side for even more "fun."

I've kept the chapters short on purpose—if you're bored, move on; if you're not, read it and smile. I'm not sure you're going to learn anything about PR from this book, except this writer wannabe has loved every moment of his ride.

And it's not over yet. Happy reading.

But First, Some Big-Time Thanks

IT SEEMED LIKE A fun invitation from Marc DeLaunay, my boss at Elgin Syferd in the 1980s.

I was invited to join a group of around 10 friends at the agency for an overnight excursion on his boat. There would be plenty to eat, and lots of beer to drink. My favorite kind of party.

All I had to do was bring a sleeping bag. Sounds easy—until I remembered I didn't own one.

I quickly called my Dad. "Do you have a sleeping bag I can borrow for the weekend?" I asked. "I can do better than that," he said. "I've got your bag from growing up—want to use it?"

I knew it wouldn't be a fancy down-filled bag from REI, but how bad could it be? I had no memory of the bag, but my Dad dropped it off and I was good to go.

Time for the party. Lots of eating. Lots of drinking. Lots of laughing. And lots of bonding with some of my favorite people in the world.

At some point, we all started to lose it. It was time to snooze. Everyone grabbed their bags and started to unroll them. Beautiful, down-filled sleeping bags. It was time to unveil my piece of shit.

I was horrified by the illustrations inside the bag. Lots of cowboys and Indians—think of every bad western movie you've ever seen. Oh my God…what have I done?

Of course, it was time to give me crap.

Someone said, "Oooh, tough guy like Rambo."

"Not Rambo," said DeLaunay. "JAMBO!"

Funny stuff. Except it stuck all weekend and, in the following weeks, morphed into Janbo, my nickname for the next 40 years. Friends like Tom Phillips have managed to form a dozen versions of the name—the one I like best is Jambalaya, because of my love for Cajun food.

I can tell how long someone has known me if they call me Janbo. It still makes me smile.

This book has been in the works for a long time. But as I started to say goodbye to treasured friends and colleagues like Dave Syferd and Dan McConnell, I realized I needed to get moving on capturing these stories of my agency adventures.

So, thank you for buying this book and hopefully enjoying a laugh or two along the way. You'll learn a little bit about PR from these stories. Or not. But I won't fail if I make you smile.

A few quick words of thanks, in no particular order.

I am blessed to have a core group of wonderful friends who have always encouraged me—and always have my back. You know who you are. Thank you.

To my family, especially my two big sisters, Sandy Hiersche and Sue VanTrojen, for their constant love and support—even when I did some real goofball stuff or got away with murder with Mom and Dad. I love you.

To my two nieces, Kim Fuqua and Tammy Fuqua, and my nephew Aaron VanTrojen, I am so proud of the adults you've become. And to my brothers-in-law Ed Hiersche and Michael VanTrojen, thank you for your constant friendship and support over all these years.

My Mom passed away when I was 13, but I've always felt her love. I said goodbye to my Dad—my best friend—in 2005. When he was on the ventilator in the hospital, I bent down and whispered in his ear: "Everything that I am, and hope to be, is all because of you—I love you."

My work colleagues turned into lifelong friends. I can't imagine my world without your friendship, support and—always—laughs.

To Cris Benson, my wife for nearly 13 years but hopefully my friend forever: your unwavering support and encouragement throughout my career still means the world to me. I've always been so proud of you and what you've accomplished in your life. I learned so much from you, especially about grace. Thank you.

To steal a thought from Ron Elgin, who has written three books from his fabulous advertising career: this book is how I remember it all. If you disagree, write your own damn book.

Enjoy!

The Early Years: West Seattle

MY ROOTS ARE IN West Seattle. More specifically, a wonderful neighborhood on 41st Avenue (between Brandon and Findlay), where all the kids knew and liked each other.

Bruce Giese was my best friend growing up. Until my mom passed away and I moved to a new neighborhood at 14, Bruce and I did everything together. We sold illegal firecrackers and tried to blow up the neighborhood. Took trips to the Trick & Puzzle Store downtown to buy fake poop and hand buzzers to shock our friends. When the new Sears catalog came out, we'd scamper behind his house and look at all the photos of women in bras.

Yes, I was a pervert in training.

We took a million trips to the West Seattle Junction for ice cream at Husky. Matter of fact, the only time I got in trouble with the law was when Bruce and another friend, Kevin Mullen, offered to take me for ice cream after my Mom's funeral. We were on our way home, when they had the bright idea of lighting a firecracker and throwing it near the box office at the Granada Theater. Boom! Bruce and Kevin scattered, and I stood there like an idiot. A cop drove me home for punishment from my dad—and he was pissed.

But I have so many happy memories of the Arbow kids (especially Theresa, Pat, and Mike) across the street, Sheri and Diane Schilz next door and everyone else. All the kids prized my comic books and my gumball machine charm collection. I had a game in which Pat and Mike could win comics of their choice if they could catch a Frisbee that I purposely tossed yards over their heads. They never caught one. I was such a little shit.

My elementary school, Fairmount Park, was just down the hill. In sixth grade, I was captain of the school safety patrol and president of the student council. But lovely Durrell Trainer still wouldn't kiss me.

I would never reach that level of greatness again.

When I got to Madison Junior High, I got into a lot of fights because I was 5'2 and 90 pounds. In gym basketball I was always a designated three pointer—my shots were worth three points no matter where I was on the court. I never made it up the rope climb. Even my good friend Bryce Nevermann thought it was funny to smash my sack lunch every day.

Between junior and senior high, I grew 10 inches and added a lot more weight. My Dad even let me grow my hair longer. But I was still a wuss. West Seattle High School and a career in communications was just about to start.

You've Got to Start Somewhere

NO KID WAKES UP and says: I want to be a PR professional when I grow up.

But I've always loved to write. As a young goofball in West Seattle, that meant producing neighborhood newspapers. Most of these papers were published for a few issues...and then forgotten. I had my own printing press, so I would set the type for my short stories. My first press used rubber type. Here's one issue I recently found with my version of breaking news:

Alligators in Lake Washington

Police have found alligators in Lake Washington. So be careful the next time you sit on a log. It could bite you!

Seriously. That was it. I sold each issue for five cents. None of my neighbors bought ads, so revenue opportunities were limited. Later, I bought a real printing press that used a composing stick and metal type. I saw an ad in Popular Mechanics from Kelsey Company for a tabletop press. It sold for $50, which is $50 more than I had.

I did the usual stuff, like mowing lawns and delivering newspapers, to make money for that press. But I also got creative. I sold illegally acquired firecrackers (don't ask), my candy from Halloween (thank you, sisters Sandy and Sue) and ultimately, my upstairs bedroom (twice!) to Sue, who was afraid of spiders.

Keep in mind that my parents owned our home, yet I was able to move real estate that wasn't mine. I sold it to Sue the first time, and then she graduated high school and moved out of our home. When she left, I moved back upstairs to my old room.

When she decided she wanted to temporarily move home, she wanted the room back. Nope, but I would sell it to her. Again.

How did I get away with this? Dunno. I've always said that Sue launched my journalism career by funding my first real printing press.

But she did more than that. I started my first business which I called Rapid Printing, creating business cards, letterheads, and imprinting Christmas cards. There was nothing "rapid" about Rapid Printing. But I was a cute little kid, and my neighbors just couldn't say no.

My Mom passed away when I was only 13, and with that tragedy, my interest in printing vanished as well. But I still loved to write. I hit high school with no real idea of what I wanted to do the rest of my life.

I had several people suggest I should join the Navy upon graduation. But I couldn't swim and had a fear of the water. So, the Navy was definitely out.

I met a teacher at West Seattle High School who changed my life: Dorothy Mootafes. Miss Moo, as we called her, saw some of my writing and suggested that I join the staff of the *Chinook*, our school paper. I remember walking into Room 258, looking around and smiling.

The girls were extremely cute. That's all I cared about. I looked at Miss Moo and thought: I can do this.

She taught me to write and edit. I thought I knew what I was doing. I did not, but Miss Moo was patient with me and made me a much better writer. I eventually became an editor in my senior year—and met my high school sweetheart, Karen Anaka, working on the *Chinook*.

After WS, I was an editor at Highline College and Seattle University, and sports editor at the West Seattle Herald under my wonderful boss, Jeanne Sweeney.

So, why didn't I stay in journalism? It looked like too much work. And the money was much better in public relations. Eventually.

Fiction is Better than Truth...Sometimes

THE PROBLEM WITH COVERING sports for a weekly newspaper in your community is you should have some kind of athletic proficiency beyond bowling.

Yeah, I could bowl. Big freaking deal. I bowled junior leagues in West Seattle for ten years. Unlike the baseball axiom in which "chicks dig the long ball," I can tell you without hesitation that chicks don't dig the polyurethane ball.

But I love sports. For some reason, Jeanne Sweeney hired me as her sports editor at the West Seattle Herald. I wasn't even out of college yet. But the legendary editor and journalist asked me to join her team. I still don't know why. But thank you, Jeanne. She's the best.

I wrote one of the most self-indulgent sports columns you've ever read. Each week, it was all about me. Scott takes swimming lessons. Scott buys a weight set. Scott discovers putt- putt golf. Hard hitting journalism.

One week I was on a tight deadline. I hadn't even started my column. So, I sat down and delivered a soliloquy about a young lad I saw juggling a soccer ball on a nearby field. This was the future of U.S. Soccer, I thought. The boy and his friends would be the reason soccer would finally take off with American kids.

Beautiful. Touching. And pure bullshit. There was no little kid kicking a soccer ball. I made it up and submitted the column. Jeanne loved it. That's all I cared about.

I felt really guilty. Journalists don't make up their subjects. But who would know, right? Later, I learned it won sports column of the year for community newspapers in Washington's statewide competition. Oops. I never told Jeanne. Until now. I hope the statute of limitations has expired.

My First PR Job: Seattle Sounders

GROWING UP, I WAS a pretty mediocre athlete. I played a lot of baseball, basketball, and tennis, and I was extremely average in all three sports.

My dream was to play third base—the hot corner—for any Little League team who would have me. When I finally made a local team in West Seattle, I was booted off because I was three months too old. When I tried out at the next level, I was cut. Clearly, I couldn't hit or field. Being cute just wasn't enough.

At West Seattle High School, I made the track team, but was relegated to the JV squad. Coach White timed my first 100-yard dash at 14.5. "Seriously?" the coach said to me. I was pathetic.

I didn't really discover soccer until my high school years. Even though I wasn't good enough to consider trying out, my soccer prowess was exhibited on the playground with the other dweebs. But I loved the Seattle Sounders, who started their North American Soccer League life in Memorial Stadium before moving to the Kingdome.

I went to all of their matches and became a huge fan. So, during my junior year at Seattle University, the Sounders announced they were looking for a summer PR intern. My dream job! I applied and was interviewed by Keith Askenasi, the team's PR Director.

To this day, I'm not really sure why…but I got the job.

I would serve as PR assistant to Keith, write articles for the team program sold at the games, and work the Kingdome's press box. All for college credit and dinner at the Kingdome on match day. Pay? Uh, no.

After the 1977 season, I was called into the general manager's office. "We'd like to offer you a full-time job as Keith's assistant," said Jack Daley, general manager. The salary was $840/month, free parking, and tickets to the games. Thinking there was room to negotiate, I decided to make a counteroffer.

Jack was not happy.

"Scott, you can't see it, but there's a line of young men and women who would kill for the opportunity I'm presenting you today," he said. "This is not a negotiation. Essentially, Scott…it's take it or leave it."

"I'm your man, Jack," I said, setting a world's record for weakest and quickest negotiation ever.

But wait…I was about to start my senior year at SU. How could I pull this off?

For the 1978 season, I worked 40 hours a week with the Sounders; carried 15 credit hours per quarter (at night) for three quarters; was an editor on the campus newspaper; worked in a paint store on Saturdays; and tried to have a girlfriend. I did this for one year, almost killing myself.

I lost the girlfriend, but I got the degree and launched my career. I spent three seasons with the team.

Keith is still a friend today, 40+ years later. I asked him one time: why did you select me for the internship?

I was hoping it was for my journalism skills or knowledge of the game. Nope. "You were less of an idiot than the others I interviewed," he said.

Well, OK then.

A Failure in Goal

I LOVED WORKING FOR the Seattle Sounders, my first professional PR job.

I didn't really take up soccer until my college years, proving over time I could suck at yet another popular sport. The Sounders put up with me for three seasons. We went to Soccer Bowl in 1977—my first year—and it was all downhill from there.

I was living large, with memories to last a lifetime. Some of my favorites:

I was at the Kingdome watching a practice. Bobby Howe, assistant coach called me over from the sideline. "You're a goalie, right?" he asked. "Uh…sort of," I said. "Want to get in goal and show our boys what you can do?"

I borrowed a pair of gloves and took my place on the line. I was feeling cocky. The players gathered near the goal to watch. "Upper right," Howe said, launching a shot perfectly near the corner. I tipped the ball over the crossbar. He nodded his approval. "Lower left," he said, and struck a shot that I dove for and saved. We did this a half dozen times. "Now, I'm not going to tell you where I'm booting it," Howe said. The next 20 shots flew past me in a heartbeat. The players could not stop laughing as I would get up each time, gather the ball from the goal and let him further humiliate me. I still have the turf scars.

Our general manager, Jack Daley, had an unusual method for tracking attendance each match. He'd call me over in the press box, look at the crowd and say something like "I think we have 24,882 fans tonight." I would take down the number and hand it to the Kingdome's public address announcer to have the crowd count announced. "Isn't this wrong, Jack?" I asked. Stupid question by the young pup.

I worked with so many terrific people. We were so damn young. Most of them are still treasured friends today. A few stand out for different reasons:

I had a massive crush on Sue Tye in our ticket department. At one point, she told me that I'd look great with a perm. I was an idiot and got the perm. You tend to do stupid things for beautiful women.

Wendy Rock, who worked with assistant coach Bobby Howe, would laugh at my awful jokes—which encouraged me to keep being funny. She's become such a wonderful friend, and she's still laughing at my stupid jokes.

Dan Wright came up with many great promotions, including one in which we handed out 20,000 kazoos to try to break the Guinness record for the world's largest kazoo orchestra. We didn't.

Finally, my sister, Susan VanTrojen, who I helped land a job in our ticket department. It was the only time we got to work together. I had to treat her like a colleague and show her respect. I'm her little brother and hated that.

The Edible Chair Contest

I WAS HIRED AS the PR Coordinator for the Pacific Science Center in 1980; I was 24 years old and still pretty clueless about media relations.

My job was to generate publicity for all the exhibits and events at PSC, a beloved family-oriented "hands-on" science museum. I worked within the development department, with talented professionals like Mary Louise Shaver, Sheila Hittle, Michael Olivere, Janet Simon, and Elizabeth Stevens—a young and scrappy team of non-profit professionals.

Most of our exhibits were fun and engaging. And of course, all science-related. Except one.

"Scott, we're bringing in a traveling exhibit celebrating top chair designs from around the world," George Moynihan, PSC's director, told me in a meeting. My obvious response should have been "what the hell?" and "what does this have to do with science?" But I was young and stupid. So, I kept my mouth shut and began to brainstorm how I could promote the show.

After a few beers, I thought about everything you could do with a chair besides sitting in it. The promotional ideas were not exactly rolling out for consideration. Then I hit upon one of the strangest ideas of my career.

"What about a competition for the most delicious chair out there? Kind of an Edible Chair Contest," I offered. Mary Louise, my boss, gave me a look that screamed "Why did I hire this idiot?" but reluctantly agreed to move forward with my program.

The contest was for a single weekend. We put out the call looking for Seattle food-lovers to create delicious chairs you could eat. I thought that it would raise awareness of our chair exhibit and draw a few folks to PSC.

Bingo! We attracted 125 candidates to display their entries at PSC—and more than 10,000 kids and their parents over the two days of our edible celebration.

While I received great coverage in Seattle media, the real prize was yet to come. I did more than 175 interviews throughout the U.S. about the contest, and the Associated Press picked up the story and told our tale nationwide.

Great weekend, I thought. But in the next few days, I received a call from a producer at *Dinah!*, a syndicated morning television show, wondering if I would come to Los Angeles, appear on their show with our big winner (a cook from Red Robin), and talk about the contest and PSC.

Dinah Shore was a big deal back in those days, and her morning show was huge. But they were also cheap. The Science Center would have to pay my expenses. Amazingly, my bosses said yes, and I was off to Hollywood with my big winner to be guests on their show.

Before the taping, I was sitting in makeup and in walks Cathy Lee Crosby who played Wonder Woman in a TV movie before Lynda Carter took over the role and made it famous. She was nice and friendly, which I thought was an opening to ask her out. Not so much. After our eyes met in the makeup mirror, she gave me the "no chance in hell look," a female response I was familiar with.

The guests that day were comedian Charles Nelson Riley, Cathy Lee, and a new rising star named Patti LaBelle. I think she's done OK, career-wise.

I came on mid-show, in my awful polyester sports coat and perm. But one amazing make-up job.

The segment went great. Dinah was gracious to me. "Was this *your* idea?" she asked. Yes, I had hatched the idea, and she gave me a polite, Southern nod and smile.

For being a guest, the show sent me a piece of luggage and a huge assortment of Rice A Roni—and yes, I ate a lot of rice in the next year. But my prized souvenir was a copy of TV Guide the week it aired, with my name in the *Dinah!* listing as a guest. And the memory of Cathy Lee's disdain.

My Very Brief Comedy Career

I'VE ALWAYS TRIED TO make people laugh. I never told jokes, although my sixth grade classmate Tommy Thompson taught me one of the few jokes I ever learned. It had to do with a king, his princess daughter…and King Kong's balls. Perfect for a 12-year-old to tell his friends.

Comedy is subjective. What's funny to me might not be funny to you. I remember briefly talking to Jerry Seinfeld at the very start of his career at a Seattle comedy club. He had just finished his set, and I was headed for the door when my date made her way to the restroom. As I stood alone waiting for her return, Jerry walked up to me with a plate of pasta.

I was star struck.

"Jerry, I love *The Seinfeld Chronicles*," I said, referencing the pilot I had viewed, that went on to become *Seinfeld*. He looked at me like I was from another planet. I felt like a comedy dork.

"It's got potential," he smiled, in between mouthfuls of pasta. Potential? Yeah, I'd say. I wanted to tell him about my brief fling with stand-up comedy ten years earlier.

On a dare, I did a five minute set of "comedy" during an open mic night at the venerable G-Note Tavern in Seattle. My routine was about taking my first public shower in junior high school. It was very visual, kind of funny and worthy of a few laughs.

I was hooked. The hell with my PR career!

After a few more open mic sessions, I entered the Seattle Comedy Competition in 1982. After auditioning, I was stunned to make the top 20. What the hell? Were the judges insane?

Probably. But for the next round, I would need to perform a short set of original stuff for drunken crowds at a different venue each night.

One problem. I had a full-time job as the PR Coordinator at the Pacific Science Center. They weren't paying me to do comedy. But how tough could it be to do both?

I developed my original set, and then tested it on my best friend, Bryce Nevermann. We started hanging out in junior high, were acolytes at First Lutheran Church ("men of the cloth," we used to say), and made each other laugh on a daily basis.

But Bryce laughed at everything that came out of my mouth. Everything. Even the stuff that was cute, but not really funny. That's what buddies do, but when I took to the stage on the first night, I was just getting polite laughter.

So, I began rewriting parts of my routine during the workday at PSC, rehearsing with my office door closed, and then performing the new stuff until the wee hours of the morning.

My co-workers were very supportive and picked up some of the slack for me during that painful week. They even showed up to see my shows. One night, I was in the middle of my routine…and I just froze. I couldn't remember the bit I had written only hours before. It got very quiet in the room. All I could see was the bright light shining on me and the smoke from the audience.

Oh crap. I'm bombing. And then…magic:

"Go get 'em, Scott," a co-worker yelled out.

"Thanks, Dad," I replied. The crowd laughed, and I was rescued.

So many performers from the top 20 went on to terrific careers, including Bill Nye, who would go on to *Almost Live* and *Bill Nye, the Science Guy*. Me? I got my ass kicked that week and was eliminated.

The PSC director was pretty direct.

"Did you get that comedy stuff out of your system?" he asked me.

"Sort of," I said. But I never performed again. America is grateful.

The Only Movie in Town

IMAGINE PROMOTING A MOVIE theater that ran the same 27-minute movie hourly—every day of the week.

To Fly! was that movie, and it ran in the Pacific Science Center's IMAX Theater. Over and over. The documentary on the history of flight was for the longest time PSC's only flick. Now, there are lots of IMAX movies. But back in 1980, it was our only offering.

Because I led a lot of tours, which usually included a viewing of *To Fly!*, I'm going to estimate I saw that movie over 200 times. It was good… it just wasn't *that* good.

I needed other content.

Somehow, I talked our director into letting me stage a 10-week film festival of the Best and Worst Science Fiction Movies of All-Time. On Saturday nights at midnight.

What could possibly go wrong with this strategy? We'd price tickets at 95 cents (our sponsor was KJR 950) and use the series to promote the theater.

I talked my film expert friend, Bob Smith, into helping me program the festival. For every great sci-fi masterpiece like *Forbidden Planet*, we also offer up *Santa Claus Conquers the Martians*.

We had a packed house every Saturday night. I'm not sure how many people were sober and awake when I'd grab the microphone and welcome the crowd. Most of them we're ending their night out of drinking and debauchery with my goofy little film series.

"You suck," I heard a few times. "Get off the stage, asshole," they'd continue. I'd just wave and smile. A few times, selected film goers would toss their cookies and leave it all behind in the theater. You could tell by the smell.

At the end of the ten weeks, our director George Moynihan called me into his office.

"Your film series is over, right?" he asked. "We're not going to do that again. Right?" Right.

He assured me more IMAX movies were on the way.

Please Let Me Come Home

I'VE ALWAYS CONSIDERED AGENCIES as the major leagues of public relations. They hire the best and brightest and sell this expertise to clients.

After three years at the Pacific Science Center, I learned that Cole & Weber had an opening for an account manager in their PR group. In those days, C&W was a solid agency. Everyone wanted to work there—including me.

I was only there for a year, and I tried to escape after my second week. It just wasn't a good fit. I snuck away one afternoon to have lunch with George Moynihan, who was executive director of the Pacific Science Center, and my most recent boss.

"George, you're probably wondering why I wanted to see you," I said. "I'll get to the point. I hate my job and want to come back home to PSC."

I was hoping he would say "Yes!" and welcome me back. He looked at me for a moment and smiled.

"No, Scott," he said. "I can't do that. You've been a great asset to the Science Center, but you need to stick it out and give C&W a fair chance."

My eyes started to well up with tears. This was not the reaction I was looking for. "You need to give it at least a year," he said.

Oh God. Now what?

I returned to C&W and did some solid work over the next several months. I'll always remember an advertising/PR brand presentation with Darigold at the agency. Before we started, Hal Dixon, president of the agency, walked up to me and interrupted a conversation I was having with the client. He thrust out his hand to me and said, "Hello, I'm Hal Dixon from C&W."

The client looked confused. I returned the handshake and said, "Hello, Hal. I'm Scott Janzen and I work for you."

Awkward, yes?

After the presentation, Hal was running around the executive suite asking, "Who the hell is this Janzen guy?"

Around week 49 (I was counting), I interviewed with Ron Elgin and Dave Syferd at Elgin Kirkland Syferd. They offered me a job. I said yes.

At week 50, I gave my notice and ran like hell to their offices on Lower Queen Anne, two blocks from where I live today. As I walked in on my first day, they were changing the sign behind the receptionist desk to Elgin Syferd—their partner Terri Kirkland had left.

I stood there and smiled. ES was the hottest agency in the market. I was home.

My PR Heroes

I'M NEVER GOING TO be asked to stand up in front of colleagues at a gala event, honoring me with a lifetime achievement award. So, this book is probably a good place to honor my lifetime PR heroes. It's a pretty short list, but the impact they've had on my career is remarkable.

Dave Syferd: I used to tell him, "Dave, if I'm anything as a PR professional, it's because of you." He'd smile, shake his head, and say: "Don't put that on me, Janbo." And then we'd both laugh. What a mentor. What a professional. What a friend. Gone too soon. Loved the man and always will.

Dan McConnell: We were colleagues at DDB Seattle. Remarkable professional. Sometimes in meetings, I'd just sit there and watch him counsel a client, piping in when I thought I could add something. Every Friday at 4 p.m., he'd crank up the tunes that you could hear throughout the agency. And that laugh!

Pat Fearey: What a brilliant counselor. I learned so much about client relations from her, and as important, I learned what "professional" really means. She knew everyone in town. I always said she had a million dollar Rolodex—back when people used them—but was forever classy in her Southern way.

Tom Phillips: I was privileged to work with Tom at both Elgin Syferd and DDB Seattle. A terrific counselor and an even better friend. Some of my fondest agency memories are working and laughing with Flip—and inhaling turkey sandwiches at Bakeman's. He used to give me so much shit. And I loved every minute of it.

But I've also worked with some cool agency colleagues over the years. They've all had an impact on me, one way or another. In chronological order:

Bob Smith: Not really a PR hero—just a cool dude who has made his mark in community journalism and is the local writer I most admire. He's done the PR thing for Boeing and others, but his real love is print journalism, and he's currently executive editor with Kitsap News Group. Bob and I met at West Seattle High working on the *Chinook* student paper, went to school together at Seattle University, and he continues to laugh at all my jokes. Even when he knows they're not funny. And man, can he write! Thanks, Bob.

Mike Saunderson: My best friend in high school and college. We did everything together, from golfing to chasing girls. He was always there for me during those challenging high school years. Thank you, Mike.

Greg Carter: A terrific photographer at the West Seattle Herald who became a top market research professional—and a lifelong friend. Questions everything—and I love that. Thank you, Greg.

Roberta Shorrock: She'll always be Berta to me from our days at the Herald. Now a big-time director with NPR's Fresh Air, she introduced me to the world of the Marx Brothers and Beaver Cleaver. Thanks, Berta.

Jim McFarland: My first supervisor in my first agency job at Cole & Weber. He kept me sane in those early days. We never worked together again but stayed friends for 40 years over our love of barbecue, hot sauce and Mariners baseball. Thanks, Jim.

Marc DeLaunay: The best new business pro I've ever worked with, Marc was my boss at Elgin Syferd. Marc and his brother Pete were largely responsible for me coming to ES. After I found out I wasn't being promoted to VP, Marc shoved his intoxicated friend into his Alfa, and got me safely to a post-function at his home where I passed out in his bedroom, and then he got me home. Thanks, Marc.

Katie Bender: My agency colleague at ES and future roommate. Loved this woman and her dog, Liza. A disapproving look and eyeroll from Katie were sometimes all I needed to make the right call for a client—or in my personal life. Thanks, Katie.

Nancy Howell: I knew her as a media star back in the day at ES—she now has Ph.D. after her name as a professor at Alabama. She befriended me early on, could always make me laugh and opened my eyes to the wonder of Patsy Cline. Thanks, Nancy.

Terry Polyak: Developed fun and powerful promotional ideas for Holland America and other clients and is still providing business counsel today. And he's always just a phone call away. A true friend. Thanks, Terry.

Scott Manning: Still calls me Starving Dog to this day (don't ask). Always provided sound counsel to McDonald's and other clients and could always make me laugh. When he shaved off his beard, I almost didn't recognize him. Thanks, Scott.

Doug Siefkes: The best B2B PR pro I've ever worked with. Loves trucks and everything about them. Taught me the best day of any week is a day that finds him with a fishing pole in his hands. Thanks, Doug.

Michael Flynn: Clients loved Michael because of his great ideas and sound counsel. On a trip together to a conference in Banff, I told him that in the coming year, I would meet the love of my life. He thought I was nuts—but I did. Thanks, Michael.

Tim Brennan: A terrific marketing pro at Fearey who did a lot of our corporate work. Would call me out on stupid concepts and was usually right. I hated him for that. Still a great friend today. Thanks, Tim.

Erica Perez: The best hair in the business. But more importantly, a solid PR professional who always delivered wonderful work for our clients—from Old Navy to 7-Eleven. And her laugh! Thanks, Erica.

Tim Pavish: An outstanding advertising pro who said goodbye to the agency game and is now executive director of the WSU Alumni Association. I love working with smart people, and Tim was all that and more. Taught me to always wear laced dress shoes and keep 'em shined. Thanks, Tim.

Dan Miller: One of those PR professionals who always "gets it"—as solid as they come. Worked with Dan on a lot of business. I never won a Totem Award until Dan showed me how—then I won three in a row. Thanks, Dan.

Heidi Happonen: We were teamed together on a lot of business—all of it successful. Watching her grow as a PR professional is one of the highlights of my career. Could call BS on me in a moment and was usually right. And then we'd laugh. Thanks, Heidi.

Jerry May: Worked with him at WONGDOODY, and then I recruited him to Destination Marketing. What a smart guy. Always found a way to make everything better—and clients happier. Thanks, Jerry.

Chris Settle: I first met Chris when he had his own design agency. We stayed friends and he got my butt to Destination Marketing. Told me it would be an adventure. It was, but fun all the way. Thanks, Chris.

Tim Hunter: We met when he was an on-air personality at KLSY and other Seattle radio stations. A terrific writer and funny guy who made life better at Destination Marketing. And he loves mushroom chicken. Thanks, Tim.

Scott Burns: One of the most creative audio pros I've ever met. I used to listen to Scott on any number of Seattle radio stations and marveled at his talent. And then I got to work with him and laugh every day. Thanks, Scott.

I know I'm leaving people out. That's the danger of a list like this. But all these people have touched my career, one way or another. So again, thank you.

The Bartlett Years

I MET BARRY BARTLETT at my first PR job with the Seattle Sounders. After my internship, Barry replaced me as the team's intern, and I started my paid assistant role.

I greeted him for the first time in the Sounders offices, and then promptly went on vacation. I was always a master of timing.

Little did I know this would start a 40-year working relationship and friendship. After the Sounders, we never worked at the same place again, but through The Bartlett Group and Janzen & Associates, Barry and I have teamed on a lot of business.

He's as good a media relations pro as I've ever worked with, generating print, broadcast and online coverage for clients. Barry brought me in to assist on many of his event clients, from interesting projects like the Northwest Flower & Garden Show to not so interesting clients like the RV Show at the Tacoma Dome.

Nothing says exciting like setting up for a live morning news segment at 4 a.m. among a dome full of RVs.

Barry and I even lived together twice. The first time, in a duplex on Queen Anne; the second, in a tacky apartment at Yarrow Bay in Kirkland.

I almost burned down the apartment one night, filling the apartment full of smoke because I didn't understand the concept of the fireplace flue after a romantic date with my girlfriend.

Another time—same complex—he watched with glee from our balcony as Kirkland police interviewed me about a neighbor's car that had been damaged overnight. We both knew I wasn't guilty, but he found it funny to wave to me sitting in a patrol car at the Yarrow Bay parking lot.

I believe we've had one real disagreement in 40 years—and of course, over a woman.

It was Friday night, and we were holding court at the Queen City Grill in Belltown. Suited up and ready to strike out once again. Two ladies walked in and, for some reason, started to talk to us.

I'm guessing it had to do with all of the drinks we were consuming.

I was taking a shine to the vivacious PR pro who was there with her sister. After a bit, I recommended that we all walk down to Il Bistro at the Market. A few more cocktails followed before I excused myself for the restroom. Upon returning, Barry was mashing with my companion.

I was pissed and left for home—with Barry's car keys. Hours later, I walked out on my deck to see Barry wailing below. He was intoxicated. I was still pissed, so I threw his keys down four stories as he searched the darkness.

Funny postscript: years later, my boss ended up hiring this same woman at the agency I was working at. I recognized her instantly, but didn't say anything about our previous meeting over the five years we worked together. On my last day, I walked into her office and spilled the beans. All color left her face. I told her she was an amazing PR pro and I didn't think it was important to ever bring it up. As she thanked me for never making that night an issue, she asked:

"Whatever happened to the other guy…your friend?"

I smiled. "Not sure," I said. "But he's probably doing well."

Celebration and Destruction

I CAN'T DANCE.

Not exactly breaking news, if you've known me throughout my career. This doesn't mean I don't *love* to dance. I do. I'm just not very good at it.

My introduction to dance began in grade school at Fairmount Park Elementary. In an ongoing social experiment that still baffles me, we'd make time each week for square dancing. Do-si-do and all that. I got pretty good at the basic moves, but it's not a skillset that would transfer to my adult life.

When I started working at different Seattle agencies, I found that everyone loved to dance, especially in the 1980s. Most of my colleagues sucked just as much as I did, but when you're bouncing around to tunes like "Whip It" by Devo, does anyone really care? No.

My Elgin Syferd buddy, Tom Phillips, and I came up with a legendary party to celebrate dancing and drinking called "Bop 'Til Ya Drop," held for four consecutive years on Elliott Bay. Many of you attended. And there are many of you who can't remember if you attended or not because of all the alcohol consumed. We sold out our cruise capacity of 150 each year.

Fun times, indeed. I used to tell people: if you're not here to dance, get off my freaking boat. Except I didn't say freaking.

Tom and I would each choose a five song set of our favorite tunes midway through the cruise. Tom always favored classic songs from Elvis and other 1960s artists. I was always cueing up tunes from 1980s groups like Go West, Duran Duran and the Go-Go's. And of course, Devo.

Elgin Syferd celebrated its move to its new headquarters in the National Building on Western Avenue with a blowout event for clients and friends of the agency. Awesome party, but it got even better when the clients went home. Our PR team helped ourselves to Elgin's liquor stash, getting even more whacked. With management gone, we cranked up the tunes and decided to dance.

On the beautiful new conference room table. In our dress shoes. Not a smart idea.

The next day, Ron calls me into his office. "I heard you might know something about our damaged conference room table," he said.

My head was still throbbing from the night before. I had passed out and slept on the floor, and still reeked of alcohol.

"Who told you that?" I asked. Inside I said: Janbo…seriously. Why does it matter?

"We're going to have to refinish the table," he said. "And you guys are going to pay for it. So, who was up there with you?"

"I can't tell you that, Ron," I said. Mainly, because I wasn't sure I could remember. "Just let me know what it's going to cost."

Then, I went around and started collecting checks from my dancing PR and ad friends. I wrote one big check to cover the cost.

But every time we had a meeting in our conference room, I'd park myself at the table and smile. That was one expensive dance.

Just Don't Kill the Nun

THE ASSIGNMENT SEEMED PRETTY SIMPLE.

Fly down to Hillsboro, Oregon, and meet with the bank manager for our client Oregon First Bank. I was to interview the tellers and learn about what made OFB different from other local banks.

I rented a big Cadillac Eldorado at the airport and began my journey to Hillsboro. In an era before GPS, I was armed with a huge folding map to chart my adventure. Once I hit town, I found myself hopelessly lost and was more than 30 minutes late to my appointment.

But soon, I got lucky and spied the bank branch just ahead. Thinking I was on a regular two-way street, I floored the Eldorado and cranked the wheel left into the parking lot—and into an on-coming Ford Pinto.

Boom! I sent the Pinto into a ditch and I went crashing into an embankment. I was dazed and confused. I looked into the rear view mirror and spotted an angry mob running towards me. All they were missing were torches and pitchforks.

"That's the guy who hit the nun!" they were yelling. "You almost killed her!"

What? They opened my door and started hauling my ass out of my smashed up vehicle.

"He's guilty—that's the guy!" they continued. I knew my rental was toast, but now I thought my life was in danger.

Soon, the Hillsboro Police were on the scene.

"Uh, son…did you smash into the Pinto?" the officer asked.

"It appears so, officer," I replied.

"You realize that was a pretty stupid thing to do, right?" he continued. They transferred me to the squad car for my safety. I called Hertz to tell them I had destroyed the Eldorado.

"Our records show that you opted for our rental insurance, so you're covered, sir. Would you like us to send out another vehicle so you can complete your journey?" she asked.

"No, I made it a rule to only destroy one car per day," I said.

The nun survived, but the Pinto was a mess. My day was over. I called for a taxi to take me to the airport and escape my day from hell.

The next day I called the bank manager. "Yeah, sorry we missed you. But you're lucky," he said. "Some idiot almost killed a nun right in front of our branch."

"Really," I stammered. "What a goofball."

Let It Snow

ONE OF MY PR mantras has always been: if it's a great idea, I created it. If it sucks, blame it on someone else.

I'll blame this one my agency mentor, Dave Syferd. Mainly because I can't remember. Unfortunately, it was probably my idea.

Our client, Sun Valley, wanted to make a big deal out of the opening of the ski season with media in major west coast cities. There was plenty of fresh powdered snow for one and all. How could we get the attention of television meteorologists to give Sun Valley a plug?

While in Sun Valley for a client meeting, we decided to shovel fresh snow into plastic bags, pack them in insulated coolers full of dry ice and ship them to Los Angeles, San Francisco, Portland, and Seattle. Dave and I would split up and arrive unannounced (never a good idea) at stations with "fresh powdered snow" and hopefully get some airtime.

I got to my hotel in Los Angeles and hired a limo to cart me around to all commercial news operations in the city. To make it look authentic, I wore a big ski jacket in 75 degree L.A. heat.

Big problem out of the gate: fresh snow turns into hard ice in a cooler. So, I smashed each bag to get closer to the concept of snow. Honestly, it looked pathetic.

I arrived at the first L.A. station asking if I could see the "meteorologist in charge." The receptionist looked at my jacket and baggie of snow. "Let me call security to escort you back to the newsroom," she said.

Back in the late 1980s, it wasn't that uncommon to visit newsrooms. It would never happen today.

The security guy held up my baggie of white power and alerted the weather guy that this idiot—meaning me—had a delivery.

From that distance, it looked like fresh cut cocaine.

"Uh, no, no, no," he said, and scampered out of the newsroom, unwilling to sample the bag of "powder" I was delivering.

"It's just snow," I countered.

"You need to leave…now," the security guard said as I was pushed out of the newsroom.

"It's snowing in Sun Valley," I yelled back on the street. Nobody gave a shit.

The limo driver said, "That's a cute idea."

Back at the hotel, I called Dave. "This was a stupid idea," he said. "I'm not having any luck in Portland. We're done."

It had to be Dave's idea.

Dating for the Cause

I WAS DOING PRO bono work locally for the March of Dimes in 1985 when I was approached to participate in a unique fundraiser to generate needed funds.

Would I allow myself to be paraded on a runway in front of a room of rabid, intoxicated women and auctioned off for charity? Hell yes was my response. At 30, you tend to say yes to just about anything.

Twenty of us accepted the call to participate in the charity auction—from ex-athletes to television news personalities. And me, an account guy at Elgin Syferd.

Of course, I started to make a big deal about this at ES prior to the auction. My boss Marc DeLaunay, tired of my self-promotion around the office, threatened to gather some of my male colleagues and bid to shut me down.

"If you do anything close to that, I will leave this agency in a heart-beat," I stammered.

"You've got to do better than that threat, Janbo," he countered. It all stayed real until the day of the auction. They showed up at the Westin Seattle to cheer instead.

In the auction guide, here was my description of the dream date with Janbo:

"We'll catch an early afternoon flight to San Francisco and spend the afternoon shopping and exploring the Bay Area. Late afternoon, we'll take a harbor cruise, and then return for dinner at one of San Francisco's better restaurants. After dinner, we'll bop until we drop at Oz, a plush disco atop the Westin St. Francis Hotel. We'll return to Seattle on a 12:15 am flight for champagne under the stars at Gas Works Park."

Was I insane? Yes. First, I would be paying for the entire date package myself. Account people at ES were not making premium dollars. If I was smart, it would have been cheaper to just write a check to the MOD.

Next, how was it going to be possible to do all of my adventure in the time I had allotted—about 12 hours? Crazy planning.

Most importantly: what if nobody bid on me? Eeek.

In the brochure, this is what I provided as my hobbies: tennis, cruising on ocean liners, dancing, comedy writing, throwing parties, video production, and dining at the Dog House.

Oh yeah…that will generate screams of interest.

I was the 12th guy auctioned that night, strutting down the runway liked a scared animal. The ladies started to hoot and holler. Yes, they were intoxicated…but you're missing the point. They were cheering for me. Sort of.

Bidding started at $100. The winner bid $1,200 for me. It turned out to be one of the high bids of the night. I took a rose and walked up to her to thank her for her generous donation and to discuss our adventure.

"You seem to be a sweetheart, but you're just a tax deduction for me," she said. "I won't be joining you in San Francisco."

Story of my life.

The next year I was back with a 24-hour trip to Las Vegas. Essentially flying down, gambling, drinking, show, drinking, dinner, drinking, and unlimited shrimp cocktails. Oh, and there would be drinking, too. As I presented the rose to the $1,500 winner, she told me "We're gonna party our brains out."

And we did. We had a very fun time, but alas, no love connection. I could hardly break her away from the slots.

I retired from competitive auction dating after Vegas.

My Evening with Donna

IT'S ALWAYS DANGEROUS TO grant a media exclusive. In return for exclusive rights to an interview subject, you're hoping the media outlet will play it up big and give your client a lot of glorious press coverage.

But if something goes wrong, you're screwed.

I developed the PR kickoff for the flagship Old Navy store in downtown Seattle—at the time, the second largest store in the U.S. We developed a week of hype and hoopla that frankly was a bit ridiculous, including a parade up Pine Street with the UW Marching Band, antique cars and 1990s soap star Morgan Fairchild. Free Old Navy jeans to the first 1,000 people in line opening day. And a VIP party the night before with a concert by the disco diva herself, Donna Summer.

Her representatives told me early on that Summer would do one, and only one, interview in Seattle. When word leaked out about the concert, I was badgered by lots of media outlets. Everyone wanted to talk to her. I chose KING TV's *Evening* for the exclusive. They promised a bundle: a crew would spend the day at the store, shooting video and doing a whole show on the opening. The crew would film part of the concert, interview Summer and provide Old Navy with 30 minutes of promotional joy.

After a day of shooting, the crew set up near the stage for her concert. Our party was kicking ass, with our guests enjoying lots of drinks and hors d'oeuvres. I was posted near the stage with my headset on, waving to friends and trying to act important.

Donna came out and started to blow the audience away with her greatest hits. A good time was being had by all. As she was performing my favorite song, "This Time I Know It's for Real," my headset buzzed.

It was her publicist.

"Donna told me before the show she's not going to do the interview. Sorry."

At that point I looked across the room. The *Evening* reporter was smiling and gave me a thumbs up. The smile would be short lived.

Despite my arguing with the publicist, Donna escaped from the stage after her final number and jumped into her limo. The KING TV crew was confused. I was angry. "You've got to tell KING," I told her representative.

The station was pissed. The Old Navy segments never aired. To try and save face, I sent a dozen roses the next day to the producer and a dozen more to the reporter. I begged for their forgiveness. I didn't get it.

But I had a happy client for all of the grand opening exposure we received. "You nailed it," he said. But how about our missing diva? "She put on a great show," he smiled. "Our guests rocked out. Sometimes, that's enough."

Not Every Idea Works

THERE'S A GREAT SCENE in the movie *Major League*. Ricky Vaughn (Charlie Sheen) is brought into a game in relief. His first pitch isn't even close, flying all the way to the backstop.

Play-by-play announcer Harry Doyle (Bob Uecker) utters "Juuuuuuust a bit outside." As were the next seven pitches.

I've thrown several terrific innings in my PR career. But I've also tossed a few that were less than stellar. They weren't bad programs, necessarily.

Just a bit outside. Some examples:

Shurgard's Key to Paradise: For the national leader in self-storage, I developed a local program for client Patti Parrish where we gave away a few hundred storage locker keys. We asked you to show up and try your key to open a unit—if it did, you won a trip to "paradise" (Hawaii). It takes a lot for consumers to stop everything and visit a self-storage facility. This wasn't it.

The Great Lottery Charity Scratch-Off: To promote Lottery Scratch tickets, I developed a one-time game show at Seattle's Rainier Square. We'd invite representatives from local non-profits and give each participant 1,000 tickets to scratch. The non-profits kept all the money they scratched, with a minimum of $1,000. Somehow, Rainier Square's Dawn Zimmerman thought this was a fun idea and approved our program. We drew a nice lunchtime crowd, but there is nothing more boring than watching people scratch tickets for an hour. Even with a possible $50,000 prize, nobody scratched more than $2,000.

Trupanion's Cone of Joy: I always felt bad for dogs and cats who were forced to wear the protective collars ("cones of shame") after a medical procedure. But what if they were cooler looking? We issued a national call to pet owners to design a fun cone their dog or cat would be proud to wear. At the last minute, I was talked into renaming the contest "Cone of Joy" versus "Cone of Shame." Everyone thought it was a cute idea, but we never got more than 50 entries despite our social and PR campaign.

Water ski lessons from O'Brien: I was asked to produce a series of ghost-written articles for a popular water ski magazine. I'd interview O'Brien champion skiers, and turn their thoughts into tips for weekend athletes, under their byline. Two problems here: 1) I'd never been on water skis because 2) I can't swim. I pray that my series didn't kill anyone.

Love at the Ballpark: For Kiss.com (online dating), I sold the client on the idea that because of baseball's slower pace, there was no better place to fall in love than at the ballpark. Sounds reasonable. I found a local relationship expert to agree with the concept. We pitched the story to Seattle media and got a few to bite. KING TV wanted a real-life example, so Cheryl Thompson, an account person at DDB, agree to fake a date for the camera. Everyone was happy.

Massage for the Military: For client Massage Envy, I created a program to provide free one-hour massages for past or present members of our armed forces. Massage for the Military would be offered over a designated weekend until all slots were filled at ME's 30+ Puget Sound locations. It was too popular. We filled up all available appointments in a few days. And I was left to deal with angry military members who couldn't get a massage. In subsequent years, we expanded the program.

Running with the Chicken

I'VE ALWAYS LOVED THE SAN DIEGO CHICKEN.

He's had many names over the years, but he'll always be just The Chicken to me. Ted Giannoulas, who has played the loveable sports mascot for more than 40 years, has entertained major and minor league baseball fans with his wild and goofy antics.

The Chicken was coming to Seattle to entertain Mariners fans, and I was assigned to generate advanced media coverage for his appearance. Anything to distract Seattle fans from some really bad baseball in the Kingdome.

First, he had to be picked up from the airport. Ted was traveling with his assistant/bodyguard, but how would I recognize him at the luggage carousel? He was never seen out of his chicken suit. A sign that said "Chicken" was not going to cut it.

I held up a sign that said "Giannoulas." A short Greek-looking man walked up to me. "You spelled my name wrong," he said. I was horrified. "Kidding!" he laughed. I was one of the few people who had ever seen him without his costume in the 1980s. But for me, this was a big deal. The three of us stuffed ourselves into my Chevette as we made our way to his Seattle hotel.

I had set up a number of radio and television interviews to promote his game appearance the next way. I arrived at his hotel with a limo, and he waddled inside in full costume. I said hello, but he only nodded his giant beak in my direction.

We arrived at KOMO AM for our first interview. When we walked in, every staffer was a kid again and wanted to high five the much beloved Chicken. But what I didn't realize—and nobody bothered to tell me—is that the Chicken never speaks in costume. Which kind of sucks for radio interviews.

The host did his best. He'd ask a question, and the Chicken would just gesture and bob around. Great for TV. Not so great for radio.

I am so screwed, I thought. But the host made light of it, and promoted the game and the Chicken's upcoming appearance.

When we left the studio, the limo was nowhere in sight. The driver had found a new parking spot a block away. But before we could plot our escape, we were spotted by…KIDS!

They came charging after their hero. We started to sprint to the limo as the kids chased us down the street. It felt like Beatlemania, except I wasn't running with John, Paul, George, and Ringo, but with a guy in a rubber chicken suit.

We got to the limo and I dove inside. The Chicken stayed behind and greeted his young fans, making some happy memories.

After his greetings, The Chicken climbed into the limo and turned to me. "Next?" he said.

For the Love of Vomit

THE TRADITION STARTED AT Elgin Syferd and ultimately carried over to DDB Seattle: the annual agency summer cruise.

The formula wasn't complicated. Ron and Dave would charter one of the Argosy boats, and we'd hit Elliott Bay for some inappropriate drinking, eating and great tunes. Our HR director would hand out cab slips at the end of the cruise for safe travel home.

Of course, there were always colleagues who drank way too much. Including our advertising and PR interns.

Actually, our interns were probably the most experienced drinkers on board, coming fresh out of school. The agency cruise was a great opportunity to relax and make their individual cases for future employment with the firm.

One year, we did an odds board, much like a Vegas sports book, of which intern would vomit first. We usually had a dozen interns at any one time, so this was a big honor if you were better than even money to toss your cookies at sea.

We all thought this was funny. And it was, actually. But everything inappropriate was funny in the 1980s.

I was up on deck chatting with Ron and Dave, along with their wives Bonnie and Trudy. It was all going quite well until I spotted trouble out of the corner of my eye.

Potential vomiting intern at twelve o'clock!

The wobbly advertising intern started to approach, barely able to stand. "I want to talk to Ron and Dave," she said to me. "I wanna work at Elgin Syferd."

I grabbed her and turned her away. "This is probably not a good time for that," I said. I suggested she sit down, but she was having none of my counsel.

She executed a perfect spin move and headed toward the management team. What happened next was not pretty. Her vomit eruption was headed towards Trudy Syferd. I threw myself between Trudy and the intern. Maybe the most heroic thing I've ever done. I got a partial hit, but I saved my mentor's wife from disaster.

After that experience, you had to be 21 to drink on the agency cruise. And no, she never worked at Elgin Syferd.

Unfortunately, she wasn't even a favorite on our intern tote board. But I emerged a hero.

Another Cocktail, Please

AGENCY PEOPLE LIKE TO drink. I don't think I'm revealing any huge secret here.

I remember watching *Mad Men* about life on Madison Avenue in the 1960s, where every exec had a bar in their office. When I started my agency career in the 1980s, in-office consumption was mostly gone. Mostly.

We'd just take our bad habits to our favorite watering holes in Downtown Seattle, Pioneer Square, and Queen Anne.

Who didn't love Tlaquepaque, a Mexican restaurant and bar near Elgin Syferd, BPN, and other agencies? I don't remember much about the food, but I do remember the tequila slammers. One night, hanging out on their upper balcony with many of my ES colleagues, I spied a bachelorette party below that just wasn't having any fun. I stumbled downstairs, introduced myself, and bought 20 shots of Cuervo to liven the party up.

They invited me to stand on one of their seats as they chanted "We love Scott…we love Scott." Once I closed out the tab, the loving stopped. Ron Elgin, watching the proceedings, gave me a thumbs-up. It was worth it. Of course, because of the expense, I didn't eat for a week, but what the hell.

When we had more ambition, we'd head down to any number of haunts, including Triples on Lake Union or Ray's Boathouse in Shilshole. For me, these places had three things in common: a) water view from their respective decks; b) great happy hour prices; and c) the opportunity to go down swinging with unimpressed ladies who realized I had a Gold Card but no game.

It didn't take long. Trust me.

My best memory was visiting Jake O'Shaughnessy's on Lower Queen Anne with some agency pals on St. Patrick's Day. I showed up in a Gumby costume because he was green, and I figured: who wouldn't want to buy Gumby a drink?

I got very drunk—surprise—and was interviewed in a live spot on KOMO TV. "Why are you here, Gumby?" the reporter asked. I just kept repeating: "I am Gumby, damn it."

I stumbled to my apartment a few blocks away, stopping at the neighborhood KFC for a bucket of chicken. After scarfing most of the bucket, I passed out on my couch.

The next morning, still dressed as Gumby, I awoke with greasy chicken bones all over me and my living room floor. Not one of my shining moments.

The Agency Contract Dance

WHEN IT COMES TO compensation, agencies are often ridiculous in what they ask for in return for what they deliver.

A few years ago at Trupanion, the first thing I was asked to do was review our contract with Edelman Seattle. Having almost always been on the agency side, it was interesting to review our contract as the client.

I kept cleaning my reading glasses to make sure I was reading the contract correctly. Were we getting a good deal having Edelman on board for both our PR and social media? Uh…no. Not even close.

After reviewing the numbers, the next part of the contract I reviewed was our out-clause, which was 90 days. At the end of my first three months, Edelman received their 90 day notice. They were not happy to be losing some major income.

It's an old adage, but the day you win a piece of business is one day closer to the day you'll lose that same business. But I have major respect for those new business experts who can source revenue opportunities and help agencies win new accounts.

The best I ever worked with was Michael Hoffman at WONGDOODY, a creative powerhouse with offices in Seattle and Los Angeles. Michael and I had many conversations about new business. It was at a time (early 2000s) in which agencies could be a bit full of themselves about compensation. I remember when Michael told me he was only really interested in clients who brought in a minimum of $50,000 of income per month.

Yet I remember WD chasing the Moneytree account, a company offering payday loans at ridiculous interest rates with advertising featuring Bob, the Moneytree caterpillar. In the pitch, I offered up community relations programs designed to soften their market image—featuring the damn caterpillar.

We didn't win the account.

PR firms look at compensation differently. Our income is mostly from professional fees, not media commissions or creative charges.

When asked "What do you charge?" it's not quite "What's your damn budget?"—but I've gotten awfully creative at times. Back in the dot com era, there were local firms who worked for equity instead of cash—and suffered the consequences when the boom went to bust.

Cash rules.

I'm equally interested in working with clients who pay their bills. I did some work years ago for a local boat show, and because we didn't get the kind of media coverage he wanted, they didn't want to pay the bill—a whopping $6,000. Still, it's the only time I've been stiffed on an agency invoice in 40 years. And ultimately, I got them to pay half of the total.

Today, I'm much better protected by contracts and letters of agreement. Also, I can recognize potential asshole clients much quicker.

My Worst Intern Ever

IF YOU'RE AN UNPAID agency intern and you're so bad you get fired, you must really suck. Let me tell you the story of Scott (not me!), the worst intern ever.

For a short time at DDB Seattle, I was put in charge of our internship program. That decision should have been questioned immediately...but what the hell, I thought. How tough can it be to find great interns?

Typically, interns are still in college and about to graduate. Or they've got their degree and are looking for that first great opportunity.

Scott was different. He was in his early 30s and had been a radio personality in Sun Valley. For some reason, he wanted to cross over into public relations. My first thought was that he was probably a bad DJ, and this was the career transition he needed. I didn't want to interview him, but he groveled, begging for a chance. What the hell.

His interview was solid. He had a pretty good skill set. I could tell he wanted the chance, but he kept looking over my shoulder at many of my female colleagues.

"How do you get any work done around here?" he asked. That should have been my signal to punt his ass out the conference room door. But we were desperate, and he was available.

I hired him.

It took less than a week for it to all go sideways. Scott liked hanging out with the other male staffers, talking sports and women. He didn't want to work very hard.

Maybe he can last the 12 weeks, I thought. Nope.

One afternoon, several my female colleagues marched into my office. They were not happy.

"Did you hire this clown?" was the initial question. They outlined several days of totally inappropriate behavior by our new intern. The only thing missing were weapons and ammunition. They were pissed.

I cringed when they outlined what he'd been up to in only three days. "You need to fire his ass—now!" one remarked.

I went to Stephanie Pearson, head of human resources. She said I should immediately let him go. I asked if she would do it.

Her look to me said: this is your mess, Janbo.

Crap.

I called Scott into a conference room. "We're going to have to part company, Scott. This isn't going to work out," I said.

For the next hour, he sobbed and begged for forgiveness. "Please, give me another chance," he said. Stephanie had recommended bringing a box of tissues to the meeting. He emptied the box in a heartbeat.

"I've only been here three days," he said. "You can't let me go."

I can. And I did. The only time I've ever fired an intern.

What did I learn? The obvious, of course. But also, to always make sure someone else oversees the agency internship program.

My Alaska Adventure

WHEN DAVE SYFERD TOOK me off the Sun Valley account at ES, he had another travel client in mind.

"You're going to be the PR account supervisor on our new Holland America Line business," he said. I had no idea what that meant.

He tossed me one of their cruise brochures.

"Oh God…no," was my initial response. "Isn't this like the Love Boat?" I asked. Dave gave me the don't be stupid look.

"It's much, much better, Janbo," he said. "One day you'll thank me for this."

As of 2021, I've taken 37 cruises in the Caribbean, Mexico, South America, and Alaska. Yes, Dave…thank you indeed.

The first 12 cruises were travel writer FAM trips, in which I played host to an ever-changing group of journalists for a week at a time. My job was to make sure they had an amazing time, and facilitate any interview requests or shore excursions. And to make sure their wine glasses were never empty at dinner.

Trust me, they were never empty.

Through all of these trips I had some wonderful experiences. I got better at it as time went on. No media request was crazy. In Alaska, want to visit the majestic Mendenhall Glacier? Sure. Enjoy a dogsled adventure in Juneau? Yep. Take a helicopter ride to the top of a glacier? You betcha.

On my first trip to Alaska, we were set to fly home from Anchorage. I hosted a goodbye dinner at the hotel restaurant and thought…this ain't that tough.

After dinner, I stood up and made a toast to my travel journalists. "Thank you for a memorable and enjoyable week," I said.

A columnist from Phoenix interrupted me.

"We're not ready to call it a trip just yet," he said. He surveyed the room. "We want to go to the Great Alaskan Bush Company."

I was 25 and stupid—and had no idea what that meant. The writers all started to chant "Bush Company, Bush Company."

"It's like *Flashdance*," my Phoenix columnist said. "Except everyone is naked."

I was so screwed. I tried to talk them into enjoying a nightcap in the hotel lounge. Nope. The wanted the Bush Company. And I was pretty sure I'd be fired for arranging an excursion—if my client found out.

They talked me into having a hotel van take us there. As we arrived, I said "You have to promise me that nothing about this excursion will appear in your stories." They all nodded yes. This was still not a smart idea, I thought.

I plunked down my agency credit card to cover the admission fees. "Want to keep this open for drinks and dances?" the hostess asked. I nodded in the affirmative.

For the next couple of hours, my writers were hooting and hollering—even the women. I kept thinking, Janbo…you have made a huge error in judgement.

The only connection to *Flashdance* was the lighting and other special effects. I was not having a good time. My writers were ordering lots of drinks and dances. My American Express card was screaming for mercy.

Finally, they had enough. It was time to go back to the hotel. The tab was around $1,200. How the hell will I turn this into the client?

The next morning, I got everyone on their respective planes, and then I flew back to Seattle. For the next few weeks, all I could think about was that my client would balk at the ridiculous expense report I had turned in. My cruise career was over.

Upon my return, the client visited our offices. As we were saying our goodbyes, Bob Brennan—the number two exec at HAL—motioned me to join him off to the side.

"How was the FAM trip?" asked Bob.

"Uh…everyone had a great time," I said. "How was the Bush Company?" he said.

Busted. My heart started pounding hard and fast.

"I saw your expense report. Are we going to see great stories on our Alaska product?" Bob continued. I nodded. "And nothing on the Bush Company?"

I shuffled and looked at my shoes. "We did a pinky swear," I said. Bob grinned and slapped me on the back.

"Good man," he said. And true to my nightly prayer requests, HAL received excellent stories. With no mention of our *Flashdance* adventure.

Never did that again.

Sometimes, Five Days is Forever

YOU'LL NEVER SEE IT on my resume, but my shortest stint at a Seattle agency was five days. You want to forget those kinds of hellish experiences. But I can't.

Back in the early 1990s, I was being pursued by a hot local PR firm—they will remain nameless. Great clients. Dazzling downtown offices. And a dynamic leader who was a knowledgeable, experienced PR pro.

They had an opening for a general manager, and I decided to go for it. To my surprise, they showed lots of interest. The employment dance began.

The duo dazzled me. Over lunch, they offered me the moon: title, awesome salary, and an office overlooking Elliott Bay. I said yes. What could go wrong?

Their publicity machine went nuts. I received all kinds of business trade media coverage before my first day. Again…what could go wrong?

On Monday, I walked into their offices ready to kick some ass. They had arranged one-on-one interviews with my new team.

The majority of the employee sessions did not go well. One by one, they told me they were not happy at the agency, and they put me on notice they were out of there unless there were big changes. Complaints includes being overworked/underpaid and a not-so-positive work environment.

I listened carefully, but I thought: how bad can it really be?

Bad. Morale was horrible. It felt like a morgue.

One incident stood out. A young account coordinator was being belittled and yelled at by the national president, in Seattle for a visit. I witnessed all of this from my office and thought: this is bullshit.

I marched out. "Don't do that," I said to our visitor, realizing I was potentially writing my own obituary.

"Who the hell do you think you are?" he asked me.

"I believe I'm your GM…please show her some respect," I answered, as he waved me off and left the office.

On Friday, I was relieved it was the end of my first week. I could gather my thoughts and enjoy a Husky Football game the next day.

At the game, my pager went off—yes, back in the old pre-cell days. I called in and I was ordered to leave the game and get into our offices immediately. Big emergency, I was told.

I soon arrived downtown. I walked in and almost everyone was at their desks, working on various projects.

"OK…what's the emergency?" I asked.

"We just need you here," I was told. I looked around the office—I was pissed. Asking me to leave a Husky game at halftime was the last straw.

Monday morning, I walked into her office of our Seattle president.

"I'm resigning from the firm," I told her. She was not happy.

I gave her all of my reasons why: disgruntled employees, horrible morale…and honestly, pretty ordinary work at expensive hourly rates to clients.

"But you've only been here a week!" she countered. "We've gotten all kinds of press on you."

"Whether it's a week, a month, or a year—I would be looking for an exit," I said. "Better to do it now before I'm introduced to clients and the rest of the company."

And then I walked out the door. Like an idiot, I told them they didn't owe me anything for the week.

I went to a nearby park and just stared out at the same body of water that looks much better from a downtown office building. Quitting on principle might sound noble. But I was now unemployed.

I soon received a call from Pat Fearey, president and CEO of The Fearey Group.

"I heard the news," she said. "Are you ready to come work for me?"

"Oh, hell yes," I said.

"Let me rephrase the question," she said. "Do you want to be part of my team…or do you want to come here because there's nothing else out there?"

I smiled. Pat knew me well. Honestly, a little of both. That phone call led to six glorious years with her agency and a friendship that carries on to today.

Thanks for saving my ass, Pat.

The Gig of a Lifetime

YOU NEVER KNOW WHEN you're about to embark on the coolest PR initiative ever.

In 1996, the Stouffer Madison Hotel in Seattle was about to rebrand as a Renaissance Hotel, part of the huge international hotel group. But what does Renaissance mean for the average Seattle employee?

Upscale, sure. World-class, yep. But how could we make the new brand come alive for everyone—from the front desk to housekeeping?

At Fearey, I came up with an idea: The Renaissance Ambassador Program. Through an essay contest, employees could talk about what it takes to be a world-class property like Renaissance. Senior Seattle hotel staff would pick a winner to travel throughout Europe and Asia, visiting eight properties to see the brand in action.

Kelly, a young hotel concierge, won the once-in-a-lifetime trip. I offered up to management that we could ask the different properties to shoot video of Kelly's travels and send the video to Seattle, where we'd edit the footage.

The GM didn't quite like the video idea. "What if you accompanied Kelly on the trip and shot the footage?" she asked.

Ding ding ding…we have a winner.

But I'd be gone for 24 days. The hotel's fees with Fearey weren't that large. How do I pull this off?

I knew I had one shot presenting this idea to Pat Fearey, my boss. I practiced my pitch for several hours in front of a mirror. It was an off-shoot of the "win-win" variety: wonderful program for the client—and we make a sizable fee for my video prowess and supervision.

I presented the idea to Pat. My heart was racing. I began to sweat and shuffle back and forth.

Pat sat there and smiled a little smile.

"If I say no, you're going to hate me for the rest of your life, right?" she said.

"Well, sort of…not really…whatever you think, Pat" I stammered. What complete BS from me. Please let me go, I thought.

"Have fun," she said. How could I not? Kelly and I spent nearly a month visiting Tokyo, Bangkok, Seoul, Amsterdam, Hamburg, Vienna, Zurich and the flagship New York property. We met with hotel GM's and a wide range of employees in each city. I shot Kelly's interactions on my video camera, but also included footage of the wonderful side activities. A horse carriage ride to dinner in Vienna; floating down a canal in Amsterdam; the Grand Palace in Bangkok; and an introduction to Seoul's exotic cuisine.

But nobody told me my duties also included being a guardian/ watchdog for my young Seattle concierge companion.

On our first night in Tokyo, hotel sales staff took us out to a bustling dance club. There was dancing and a lot of drinking. At one point, I looked at my watch and saw it was getting late. Kelly and I had an introductory meeting the next morning with the hotel GM.

"We need to get back to the hotel and get some sleep," I said.

She looked at me and said "No." The sales team looked at me kind of funny.

"Really Kelly…we need to go back," I said.

"I'm not ready to go back," she said. Our first standoff.

"We'll take good care of Kelly and get her back to the hotel," they said.

I knew I was going to lose this battle. Reluctantly, I agreed to the terms of the exchange and went back to the hotel.

The next morning, Kelly met me in the lobby, her eyes weary and red from her dancing adventures.

"Kelly, we can't do the tour like this," I said. I felt like a grandpa, even though I was only 41 years old. "You're representing the Seattle property, and I'm responsible for your behavior and safety. I will cancel this trip right now if we can't agree to this."

She smiled at me. "You wouldn't cancel this trip," she said. Kelly knew I was bluffing.

"Watch me," I said. What utter crap.

Her behavior improved, although there were a couple of relapses later in the trip. I was able to shoot some terrific footage, and we produced a cool video that won an international travel PR award.

When we arrived back in Seattle, the GM pulled me aside. "Honestly, Scott…how did Kelly do?" she asked. I promised a full debrief the following week.

At the client session, I had a big decision to make. We got the footage and generated some amazing publicity throughout Europe, Asia and here in Seattle. Do I still bust her ass, I wondered?

"She was great," I said. "A total professional, and a wonderful representative of this hotel."

I think I saved her job. But for the PR gig of a lifetime, I felt it was OK to lie a little. OK…lie a lot.

All Hail the Slurpee

AT THE FEAREY GROUP, I managed the Southland Corporation account for Washington/Oregon—or as we all know it, 7-Eleven.

As a kid, I used to bicycle to my neighborhood store for yet another Coke Slurpee. I lived for brain freezes. Which of course could explain my lack of mental prowess growing up. But that's another story.

When we captured the regional promotional business for 7-Eleven, I was pretty happy. My role was to develop and negotiate radio promotions, primarily in Seattle and Portland.

My partner was Erica Perez, who moved on from motivating consumers to race in for Slurpees and Big Bites to a successful PR career at area agencies, including her current firm in Portland.

Most people don't visit their local 7-Eleven for their nutritious weekly groceries. It's all about hot dogs, pizza, wings, nachos…and Slurpees.

The company provided me with pads of coupons of their food offerings to distribute to media and other influencers. Almost none of these coupons ever made their way to local reporters.

I used them to feed our younger staff.

I felt like Marlon Brando's character from *The Godfather*. As it got near lunchtime, our interns and account coordinators would happen by my office. They weren't there to say hello. I would wave them in,

"How can I help you today?" I'd ask.

I would dispense the coupons, and they would be fed for another day. My only request was that they go to different 7-Elevens or the client would get suspicious. I couldn't use the coupons because most of the store managers knew me.

People Like Free Stuff

IT'S ONE OF THE oldest PR tactics out there. To launch a new product or promote a big event, drop off goodies to local radio stations and hope their on-air personalities talk it up on the air.

It's harder to do it today because of security and pandemic concerns, but PR pros still make the rounds. I've had some funny experiences with media drop-offs.

I was part of the agency team in Seattle to promote McDonald's McDLT in the late 1980s. A bizarre cheeseburger product launch all about the Styrofoam container it came in, keeping the burger (hot) on one side and the lettuce/tomato (cool) on the other. When it was time to eat, you brought both sides together.

On launch day, we picked up McDLTs from a local franchisee, and raced to stations to drop off the samples - not really comprehending that the burgers would go cold by the time we reached station's front desks. The product and its packaging got more laughs than on-air than praise.

For a soccer ball giveaway with the Sounders, we filled a team van with our giveaway balls and headed downtown. My driver hit the brakes suddenly, springing the back door open, and freeing up a few hundred soccer balls to bounce down Fourth Avenue. Not a good thing.

To promote Old Navy's Seattle opening, we dropped off branded swag for five consecutive days. They didn't care much about days one through four, but on day five we delivered $50 gift cards. We were very popular with station receptionists that day.

But the best for *me* all-time was a scratch ticket giveaway for Washington's Lottery. We dropped off 100 tickets to each station hoping they would scratch them on air to promote our latest game. But I bought about a thousand more than needed, and afterwards stuck the extras in a prize closet at my shop.

I totally forget about the tickets until it was time to close my agency doors for good. I opened a box filled with 1,000 scratch tickets. What the hell do I do with these? I was no longer working with the Lottery, and they didn't even know I had them.

Hmmm…riches await. I took the box to my car and drove to a nearby park in Bellevue. In what felt like a drug deal, I sat by myself and scratched the misbegotten tickets. The top prize was $10,000, so there was money to be made. Ethical? No. Legal? Probably not. But screw it…it was time to scratch!

My front seat was filled with the latex residue from scratching tickets. It takes a long time to scratch so many. My guilt was huge. I kept looking out my window, wondering what I'd say to a local cop if he stopped by asking me what the hell I was up to.

Finally, I finished the adventure. No big winner. I pocketed around $150 and a sore wrist from my non-stop scratching.

I found scratch-off-ticket material in my car for years. Such is the price of crime.

The Eddie Bauer Layoff

ONCE I STARTED MY career in agency public relations, I really had no desire to go to the corporate side.

But when the Director of PR opening appeared for Eddie Bauer, I decided to check it out. In those days, I lived the brand. Not because of my outdoor prowess—I have absolutely none—but because half of my clothes came from EB. My daily uniform in 2007 was a pair of khakis and a button-down shirt underneath one of their legendary down vests. Every single day. The suits were gone.

The EB job still holds my personal record for submitting my resume/cover letter and hearing back from a recruiter—16 minutes. Was I that good, or was the company that desperate? After multiple rounds of interviews, I got the offer as I was riding Amtrak to Portland.

I was only at Eddie Bauer for a year. The company was not doing well, and layoffs were coming. But I was at the management level, so I was safe, right?

We were told of floor-by-floor meetings on a particular Friday, all happening at the same time in our Bellevue corporate office. That morning, I wandered into David Makuen's office, our VP of marketing.

"Hey, David…the rumors out there are about hundreds of layoffs happening today," I said. "Should we strategize how to position this with the business press and have a release ready to go?"

I'll never forget the look he gave me.

"Uh…it's all handled, Scott," he said. "We're all set to go."

Dead man walking, I thought, as I scurried back to my office. My team was already gathered. Anita Woo, my terrific PR Manager, asked if the team was going to lose their jobs.

"No Anita," I said. "I think it's gonna be me. I make too much money." Words I've rarely said in my career.

I was soon told David wanted to see me. When I marched back in, I knew I was screwed. He pushed a termination document towards me. I just stared at it. Maybe if I didn't read it, everything would be all right.

But I was toast, as were hundreds of my co-workers. My team was safe. But I was gone. And pissed.

After gathering my stuff, I started the ride across 520 back to Seattle. After calling my wife, Cris, to deliver the crappy news, my second call was to my financial consultant, Scott Settle. "Sell all of my shitty Eddie Bauer stock now," I said.

"You don't sound happy," Scott replied.

The stock would eventually drop to less than a dollar per share weeks later.

Agency PR was suddenly looking better again.

Swung On and Belted

I DEVELOPED CONSUMER RADIO promotions for Washington's Lottery for five years, all designed to get you to buy Scratch tickets you didn't know you needed.

The work started at BPN, and continued at my own agency, Janzen & Associates. We would leverage the radio advertising buy to obtain extra on-air exposure through goofy games I developed in conjunction with Steve Lawson, legendary producer extraordinaire.

We had a baseball-themed scratch ticket about to roll out. I thought it would be a cool idea for Steve to record fake play-by-play audio—if lucky listeners picked the right clip and the batter got the big hit, they'd win baseball-themed tickets.

I just assumed we'd use Steve as the voice talent. "What if I could get Dave Niehaus?" he asked me. As in, Dave Niehaus, legendary Mariners broadcaster and my voice of summer? That Dave Niehaus? Yes, please.

Dave agreed to our meager talent fee and entered the studio one morning. He was wearing a track suit, and just kind of shuffled in to do his work. I almost peed my pants. I had so many things I wanted to tell him and the impact his Mariners broadcasts had made on my life.

I froze in his presence, babbling something ridiculous. He just smiled, put on the headphones, and got ready to take Steve's direction.

Dave reviewed the different play-by-play scenarios, and then asked Steve if he could improvise a bit. We nodded our heads.

The next half hour was magic.

"Swung on and BELTED, deep to center field!"

"It's a double down the left field line, and it's going to score the runner from first!"

"Get out the mustard and the rye bread, Grandma! It's Grand Salami Time!"

Holy shit…I was in baseball heaven.

When Steve got the takes he needed, he told Dave we were done. Dave took off the headphones, shuffled out of the booth and left the studio.

I sat there for a moment, realizing I had witnessed greatness. When Dave made the Hall of Fame years later, his speech at Cooperstown closed with this:

"I know there are several bigger names who have preceded me in winning this award. And there will be several bigger names after me to win this award. But no one will ever be more appreciative."

I miss you, Dave. Thank you for spending 30 minutes with me in a studio. Sorry I was an idiot. You were the best.

Secondhand Smoke

I DIDN'T KNOW MUCH about Destination Marketing before I came to work for the agency. I knew it was a retail-driven shop, known for their work with Sleep Country USA, Car Toys and Lynnwood Honda, among other accounts.

They had an opening for a VP level advertising professional. I know enough about advertising to be dangerous, but I've never positioned myself as an ad pro. Yet, I was hired as their director of account services—something I *did* know a lot about.

DM was the quiet ad agency in Mountlake Terrace the marketing industry knew little about. But they kept acquiring accounts and cranking out the work. When I offered to tap my PR expertise to raise their overall visibility, it was met with a collective "meh" by the owner/CEO, Dan Voetmann. Tapping their internal audio and video production facilities, Dan was pretty happy being under the radar.

At my employment acceptance lunch—appropriately at a restaurant named Scott's—Dan asked if I could attend a new business meeting the next day for a new client, LeafFilter. They produced a gutter screen to drain water but keep the leaves and other debris out. Sure, I said, not knowing I was about to experience one of the strangest client meetings ever at their offices in the south end.

My first clue was when we stepped in their front door, and found just about everyone smoking. It seemed so strange in 2010. The receptionist had a small portable fan at her desk, but it was just blowing smoke around the room.

We were invited into the office of Mitch Reed, president/CEO of LeafFilter NW. The smoke levels in the lobby looked tame compared to Mitch's office. I'd never seen an office as smoky and toxic in my life. As we sat down, I could barely see my new DM co-workers. Mitch also had a small fan, but it was working overtime trying to clear the haze. On his desk he had what was left of a dozen doughnuts.

"Care for a treat?" Mitch offered. Uh…no.

I remember looking over at Chris Settle, our creative director and the friend who had tipped me off on the opening at DM. I couldn't see his face, but I could hear his cough.

My first thought was not about how we were going to market LeafFilter—rather, it was about dry cleaning my suit after the meeting.

As Mitch smoked cigarette after cigarette as he explained their mission, my eyes were watering as I dreamed about the clean outside air just steps from the front door.

Would they notice me if I bolted out of their offices? Only if they could see me, I thought.

Mitch was a Mad Men-era pro who loved to tell stories of his days in New York. Unfortunately, that meant this meeting would last forever. I hadn't officially started my first day at DM, but I was risking sure lung cancer if I worked on this business.

At the conclusion of the meeting, we said our goodbyes and walked towards our cars. I let out a long series of suppressed coughs, as did my colleagues. Now I could see Chris' face, and we both smiled. Are they all going to be like this, I wondered.

Chris and his team ultimately did some terrific TV and print work for LeafFilter, playing off their "Leafless in Seattle" tagline. But my dry cleaning bill was never the same.

Alas, No Brooke Shields

REMEMBER THE SYNDICATED TELEVISION show *Lifestyles of the Rich and Famous* from the 1980s? The bombastic host, Robin Leach, always invited viewers to indulge in "champagne wishes and caviar dreams."

I got a little taste of all that. The show contacted my client, Holland America Line, with a request. They wanted free passage on a 14-day Mexican Riviera cruise for an Italian designer, six models and a photography crew to document his upcoming clothing line. In Acapulco, some of his celebrity friends like Brooke Shields and assorted B-level TV actors would come on board for an event to celebrate the new fashions at a lavish party.

What would we get out of it? National television exposure. I was asked to accompany the group and facilitate all of their needs.

Wow...I get to meet Brooke Shields. Or so I thought.

At the last minute, the designer decided not to take the cruise, so I was left in charge of six models who weren't of legal drinking age and had never experienced this kind of travel adventure. What could go wrong?

On the first night, it started to get out of control. The models started to drink, dance and essentially, lose their minds. They were running all over the ship and then loudly partying in their cabins. All night long.

Normally, a dream assignment for me. But I was in charge and these ladies were determined to break every shipboard rule. And my will.

The first morning at sea, I was called into the Hotel Manager's office. For 15 minutes, he yelled at me for allowing all of this to happen. In one night, the models had essentially upset lots of passengers and crew with their antics. And I was to blame.

I took my beating from the Hotel Manager. It wasn't pretty. "If there is a repeat of last night's shameful behavior this evening, I will throw the entire entourage off the ship at our first port of call," he said.

He wasn't kidding.

I interrupted a photo shoot on the Lido Deck and called an emergency meeting of these idiots.

"Essentially, if you guys don't behave and get your shit together, the cruise is over," I said. A couple of the models started to cry, and tried to blame me for letting them loose on the ship.

I just shook my head. They wouldn't really throw us off the ship, would they? they wondered.

In a freaking heartbeat, I replied. "Uh…yeah," I said, knowing it included me.

Suddenly, they became model citizens at sea. Their days were filled with endless photo shoots, both on the ship and at our Mexican ports. When I'd see the Hotel Manager, he'd just smile and nod.

Just before we reached Acapulco, we received word that the on-board party with Brooke and company was cancelled because of the designer's absence from the cruise. Not a surprise.

Months later when the segment finally aired, we were in for a bigger surprise. In Leach's voiceover narration, the name of the cruise line and ship were not mentioned—which of course, is the reason we let those idiots on board. And Leach made it seem like the ship was the designer's own private vessel.

After I watched the show, my first and only thought was: Janzen… you're screwed.

The next week, I ran into some HAL executives who had seen the segment. "What the hell was that POS, Mr. Janzen?"

Years later, I still have no answer. The segment was worthless. The models were insane. And I still haven't met Brooke.

You Can Go Home Again

ONE OF THE THINGS I learned early in my agency career is that titles and big compensation packages really aren't that important.

Which, of course, is BS. Hell yes, they're important.

Every promotion and raise were critical in my professional growth. I *really* wanted to be a VP, until I learned that almost everyone didn't give a crap. Except me.

Pat Fearey rescued me from unemployment and hired me at her firm. I came in as an Account Supervisor before soon becoming a VP at The Fearey Group. I loved working with Pat and the team at TFG. I outlasted the two other VPs, and soon was promoted to SVP.

So far, so good. The grand master plan was for me to purchase the agency and let Pat and her husband Jack retire. But even though the occasional conversations about a succession plan, it just wasn't happening.

At the same time, my friends at DDB Seattle came a calling. DDB had acquired Elgin Syferd a few years earlier, and most of my ES friends from my six years in account services were still there—but all grown up. DDB was a glamourous global agency, and for some reason, they wanted Janbo to return.

I had a couple of secret breakfasts with Ron Elgin, my former boss and CEO. It was always great to see Ron, but I felt I was cheating on Pat Fearey. I tried to convey that I was very happy at TFG. And then he got to my enormous ego.

"We should have never let you walk out our door, Janbo," he said. "And your buddy, Tom Phillips, wants you to return."

Tom was now director of the whole PR division, and yes, one of my dear friends in the industry. "You'll come back as an SVP (ding, ding) and a leader at our shop," Ron said.

I soon got together with Tom. He came with a written offer that among other things, promised me the opportunity to work on big, national accounts with a talented crew of PR pros. The money was great, but the last line of the offer was the capper:

You'll be the starting third baseman of the DDB softball team. Ladies and gentlemen…we have a winner.

Maybe Pat had sensed something, because a few weeks earlier she had named me President of TFG. Pretty exciting stuff.

So, what's a goofball like me to do? I soon marched into Pat's office to resign. She was not happy.

"When did you stop believing in the dream?" she asked me. Words that still haunt me to this day.

But I had to go "home" to DDB. I'd be coming back a hero with the VP title I always wanted, surrounded by lifelong friends.

But I hurt and lost my special friend and mentor, Pat. It was several years before we talked again. I'm happy to say that Pat and I are friends today—even after all of the pain I caused.

I spent five years at DDB to go along with the six years I spent at ES. When I was laid off from DDB in 2005 after we lost some business, I asked credit "for time served," so I was treated as an eleven year employee for severance purposes.

Ron bankrolled a going away party for me at a downtown restaurant. When I saw the final bill, my drunken eyes grew big and I told him that next time, just cut me that check and I'll buy my friends some beers.

The 60-Second Vacation

IT SEEMED LIKE A challenging assignment: increase cruise sales in the competitive New York market for Holland America Line.

My advertising partners at DDB developed several strong creative strategies, including something called "station domination," in which we'd dominate NYC's subway station paid advertising opportunities with our messages. I was asked to develop a promotion that would complement our marketing efforts.

If you know me, you know I love to cruise. As of 2021, I've sailed 37 times throughout the Caribbean, Mexico, Alaska, and South America. There is nothing better than relaxing in a deck chair, sipping a cool drink, soaking up the rays and watching the sea roll by. What if I could offer potential cruisers the same opportunity in the cold weather of January—even for a minute? Would they consider taking a cruise?

I developed an idea called the 60-Second Vacation. I'd hire someone to build a replica deck of a cruise ship that could be transported to a NYC subway station. The deck would feature a warm weather graphic background, with deck chairs, steel drum band and heat lamps. We'd invite you to plop yourself down in a deck chair, put on a pair of sunglasses, sip a beverage, listen to the exotic sounds of the band and dream of taking a cruise of their own. A photographer would provide a souvenir photo of your 60-second adventure.

I will always remember pitching this to the HAL marketing executive.

"Have you ever done this before?" he asked.

"Uh…not quite," I answered.

"Will it work?" he followed.

"But of course," I said. The deck alone would cost $40,000 to build, I remembered. It had better work.

We shipped it to the station in the World Trade Center. And in case you're wondering: January 2001, months before our world would change forever.

The deck was set up and staffed for our two day adventure. Now, would busy (and freezing) New Yorkers care?

They did—big-time. According to the Port of New York, more than 150,000 commuters experienced our stunt over two days. We grabbed 5,000 email addresses from people who wanted more info on a HAL cruise. And the best part: 400 people got into a deck chair, closed their eyes, and dreamed of taking a cruise. As part of the overall campaign, we bumped up cruise sales in NYC.

Later, we replicated the same program at a BART station in San Francisco, but the program was too expensive to ship and staff around the country.

I love clients willing to take a risk on an unproven concept. This time…it all worked.

Singing with a Beach Boy

THE BEACH BOYS ARE one of my all-time favorite American bands. Their music was the soundtrack of my summers growing up.

Back in 1983, the Seattle Mariners developed a pretty cool idea, hosting a Beach Boys concert following one of their games. It was scheduled for the Kingdome, where great music always went to die.

To promote the show, Bruce Johnston, keyboardist for the group, would come to Seattle prior to the game for a media tour. Bruce joined the group in 1965 and would have lots of stories to dazzle local media. I was the PR account manager for the Mariners at Elgin Syferd, and it was my job to book him in as many radio and television outlets as possible.

I did well. We had him scheduled for a dozen interviews in eight hours, and my day would be crazy. We picked up Bruce at his hotel in the customary limo, but I wasn't prepared for the small entourage that crammed in as well.

I had so many questions I wanted to ask Bruce about the Beach Boys and their music. But he had lots of questions for me, instead, including the most basic:

"What's your favorite song of ours?" Bruce asked, smiling knowing it would be a difficult question to answer because I loved them all.

"Well...uh...I mean...I love 'California Girls,' 'Good Vibrations,' 'God Only Knows,' 'Surfing USA'...I could go on and on," I said. "But there's one song I love to sing..." I said.

"Sing it," Bruce replied, smiling. Uh oh, I thought. Here goes nothing.

"Ba ba ba ba Barbara Ann," I quietly sang, humbled that I was doing a horrible version of their cover hit, "Barbara Ann." But suddenly, Bruce and the rest of the limo joined in. I was singing with a Beach Boy!

"You got me rockin' and a-rollin, rockin' and a-reelin, Barbara Ann, ba ba ba ba Barbara Ann," we sang. I was in heaven.

My buddy Bryce Nevermann loved the Beach Boys as much as I did. We had a lunchtime break in the interviews, so I decided to get really bold. "My pal Bryce works at a camera store on our way," I asked. "He's a huge fan. Can we stop by and say hi?"

Bruce thought this was funny. I don't know why. We pulled over in front of the store, and I marched in with my Beach Boy. But Bryce was at lunch. Bad timing. Bruce autographed a photo ("Sorry we missed you Bryce!") and laughed our way back to the limo.

The overall media coverage was huge. The crowd for the game was huge. The sound quality was not huge. It sucked. But I'll always have Barbara Ann.

Doing the Right Thing

I BECAME OUR BEER promotional expert at DDB. Not because I drank a lot of it—which I did—but because I was pretty good at creating programs to generate sales both in-store and at restaurants and bars.

One of my beer clients once told me that "remember…you only rent beer." Which was always apparent after long beer-filled meetings with these same clients.

I created some cool programs. For Beck's, I maintained there was nothing better than a cold brew on a sunny day, so I developed "Beck's & Decks," a series of 12 parties on some of Seattle's best decks. We priced Beck's for $1 during the party. You generate a lot of trial and sales that way.

For Australia's Swan Lager we staged beach parties in the winter months (their summer is our winter), complete with surfboards, sand, and swimwear. I learned early on with beer promotion that cheap beer and goofy stunts work every time.

I was lucky enough to develop programs for other beers including Pacifico and Chihuahua. My account manager, Stan, would never indulge in any of our client's beers. I couldn't figure it out—and I couldn't drink enough beer to make up for his lack of interest. Finally, Stan whispered to me, "Scott…I don't drink. I'm a recovering alcoholic." Yet, I had him front and center on all our beer accounts. I learned at that moment to ask all the right questions up front.

DDB was approached by a new product coming into the Puget Sound market called Treaty Beer. The beer was an ordinary lager, and their goal was twisted: for every Treaty Beer sold, proceeds would go to fight Native American fishing rights.

Ron and Dave called me in to ask my thoughts.

"We can't seriously be thinking of taking these guys on, can we?" I asked. It would have brought in significant advertising and PR revenues.

I started to outline agency liabilities if we took it on. "It's racist, obnoxious…it's just plain wrong," I continued, without taking a breath. "There will be protestors outside our offices on Second Avenue. I mean… we just can't."

Dave looked at me and smiled. "Are you done, Janbo?" he asked. "We're not going to take it on."

Treaty Beer never rolled out in this market. A very good thing.

The Eddie Bauer Mississippi River Challenge

EDDIE BAUER WAS AN account of mine at Elgin Syferd, long before I went to work for the company.

In 1984 my client was approached by two champion canoeists, Valerie Fons and Verlen Kruger, who wanted to break the Guinness record for canoeing the 2,348-mile Mississippi River. EB sponsored the pair, and their journey was dubbed The Eddie Bauer Mississippi River Challenge. He was 61 and she was 33—could they really pull this off? And could I get America to care?

I was asked to orchestrate a national media relations campaign, even though my only canoe experience was attempting not to drown in Seattle's Union Bay.

Valerie and Verlen would start at Lake Itasca in Minnesota, and end in the waters south of New Orleans in the Gulf of Mexico. We'd stage media opportunities along the way in St. Louis, Memphis, and New Orleans—and hope reporters would show up.

After our kick-off at Lake Itasca, I was flying back and forth between Seattle and the next major stop on their journey. This was all pre-internet, so it was tough to get the word out to media. No cell phones, no websites, and no nothing.

I convinced hundreds of radio stations throughout the U.S. to carry produced audio segments on the journey, and we shot video that was distributed to television stations who were crazy enough to care. Even *People* magazine ran an amazing story on the world record attempt.

I told my client we would need a media boat and helicopter in the Gulf of Mexico to document their arrival. They stopped asking "how much is this going to cost?" and just went for it.

When Valerie and Verlen arrived, they had broken the Guinness record in 23 days, 10 hours, and 20 minutes. I stood on the deck of the media boat with my arms folded and just smiled.

What the hell had we just done? And how much had we spent to get it done?

Valerie and Verlen would get married a few years later—how could you spend that much time in a canoe and not? I was left with a happy memory but determined this was my first and last canoe adventure.

My Only Volcanic Eruption

ALONG THE WAY, I'VE built up strong expertise in retail public relations. I've always been fascinated by what influences people to buy the products and services they do.

Before Amazon and the whole online shopping experience, there were malls like SuperMall of the Great Northwest in Auburn. SuperMall opened in 1995, promising terrific savings—at least 30 percent—at more than 160 stores.

I was the account supervisor at The Fearey Group and charged with creating a lot of hoopla for the grand opening. My client was the wonderful Lynn Beck, marketing director, who got her start with Frederick & Nelson and would eventually become the GM of Pacific Place.

Lynn remains one of my all-time favorite clients, because she knows that true marketing magic comes from collaboration, trust and taking chances.

So, she was ready to hear my crazy ideas.

"I want our Mt. Rainier replica to erupt with fireworks when we open the doors," I offered. Check.

"I want to go a little over the top in pre-opening PR," I said. Check again.

"I want traffic to back up for miles to get to SuperMall on Opening Day." I didn't actually say that, but I thought: how cool would that be?

My Fearey team went to work. The hype machine was going nuts. Every area media outlet wanted to cover our grand opening, including all four Seattle television news stations, who parked satellite trucks in the mall's parking lot. Coverage started with the morning shows and continued all afternoon. From our media center, I watched the coverage live, including traffic copters providing images of traffic—backed up for miles. I stood there in front of the monitors feeling like I had helped create a little retail madness.

There were some interesting stores at SuperMall. Ones you'd expect (Nordstrom Rack and Saks OFF Fifth) and ones you wouldn't (Dress Barn and The Flag Store).

One aspect I was very proud of: we shared the front page of every major newspaper in the state along with the debut of Windows 95 from Microsoft.

And front and center: my erupting Mt. Rainier.

Teaching PR Writing at SVC

THERE'S NO BETTER EXAMPLE of great communications pros giving back than Seattle's School of Visual Concepts. It's a wonderful resource providing instruction in every aspect of marketing, branding and design by seasoned, working professionals.

Larry Asher and Linda Hunt run the place. It's not been easy to do, especially during the pandemic. Most recently, they had to move to an online model for obvious reasons. I look forward to the day they can offer in-person learning once again.

Larry and I first met in 1989 at BPN. He was our creative director, and I was a senior PR dweeb, working mainly on Washington's Lottery. He's extremely talented—that's a given. But it was his wiseass sense of humor that told me we'd be friends for life.

Larry eventually acquired SVC. A very smart move. He reached out and asked if I'd be interested in teaching a course on PR writing, targeted for newbies to the field.

The previous instructor had left, and Larry thought I'd be a great fit. He made it sound inviting: 10 weekly classes, three hours per class at a ridiculously bad teaching fee.

How could I say no?

Of course, it would turn out to be more than 30 hours, with homework review and one-to-one sessions with students. But I said yes, and taught at SVC for five years.

Maybe it was the idea I could develop my own curriculum, based on my career in public relations. Maybe it was the idea I had of bringing in guest pros from Seattle's PR community to provide their wisdom. Or maybe I just wanted 20 students to address me as Mr. Janzen, which previously was only used by creditors I owed money to.

Don't tell anyone…but I actually enjoyed teaching that class. The young talent that emerged are now kicking butt in PR roles throughout the region. I love that most of all.

One class from my five years stands out, but for the wrong reason. I would always bring in Dan McConnell to be my guest lecturer during crisis communications week. Dan was considered one of the top crisis pros around, and he never turned me down each quarter. My students loved Dan and his crisis stories.

It was always an easy week for me. I'd introduce Dan, and stand off to the side as he held court for an hour. But on this night, something didn't seem right. He was a big, burly guy and always ready for a welcome hug. But he seemed distracted and distant as he set up his laptop.

I just shrugged it off. Dan was perched on a stool in front of the class, and this night his presentation was not smooth at all. Soon, he started to sway back and forth on the stool for no apparent reason. I could immediately tell that my crisis pro was about to experience a crisis of his own. Dan started to lose his balance and was about to hit the floor. I rushed up and caught my big friend, shielding his fall with my body.

Boom. We both hit the deck. My students sprang into action, and helped lift Dan off of me and into a chair, calling 911 to bring on medics who determined all of this came from new meds he had started taking the same day.

Dan was embarrassed. He had no reason to feel that way. But I was pretty shaken. "I knew you wanted something different for your crisis week," he smiled. "Thanks for catching me," he said.

When the medics left, I rejoined my class. I had to assure them that Dan's fall was not part of a crisis exercise. It was tough to teach that last hour, wondering about the health of my pal.

Dan passed away a few years ago. I miss his big hugs and wonderful laugh. He was an icon.

Idiots Who Hire

MY INDUSTRY HAS A horrific record in hiring and firing young talent. Or as I've learned in the last several years, old talent.

I remember early in my career, I was told I just didn't have enough experience. As I got older, I realized I had too much.

Don't get me started about age discrimination. It's real. I started to dumb down my resume and remove relevant dates in my career and education as to not age me older than I really was. I found out that in my most recent employment in the 500+ employees at Trupanion, I was the oldest employee in my early 60s. How the hell did that happen?

Two interesting recruitments of mine from over the years stand out. Their names will not be used because they're dorks and don't deserve the exposure. In no particular order:

Agency #1: fast-rising—but kind of boring—public relations shop. I had multiple meetings with all their execs, including the president. Everyone seemed to like me. They wanted to bring me in as an SVP, and the owner even hinted at some equity. Yay. An offer was coming the following week after the standard reference check.

But suddenly, all I heard were crickets. They recalled the offer, saying they had talked with someone in the industry (not on my reference list) who thought I wasn't up for the task. Years later, I learned it was a former co-worker at DDB who was campaigning to be considered herself. When I heard all of this, I was angry. "We made a mistake listening to her," the exec later told me. No kidding.

Agency #2: traditional public affairs firm. Multiple meetings for a VP role. All the interviews went well. It was time for the offer. I got a call, asking me to come downtown that afternoon to meet with the agency president. I put on my suit and raced for their offices, giddy with anticipation.

After 15 minutes of small talk, he leaned forward at his desk. "Scott, we've really enjoyed getting to know you and learn a lot about your expertise," the president said. I'm thinking: just make me an offer. Now.

"But we're going to go with the other finalist, because she has tech experience that you don't—it's an area we want to get more involved in," he continued.

At this point, I wanted to kill him. Why did he ask me to come downtown?

"But we really like you…so, what would you think about coming to work for us as her number two?"

I cleared my throat. "With all due respect," I started. These are words you *never* want to hear me say. "With all due respect, there's no chance in hell of me working for her. We're done here," I said.

And they didn't even validate my parking.

But I balance experiences like that with my happy recruitment to Elgin Syferd as an account manager. My interviews went well, and the last session scheduled was some time with Ron Elgin and Dave Syferd.

Very relaxed. They asked great questions. After about an hour, Dave left the room and brought in cold beers for the three of us. "I like this guy. He doesn't appear to be an asshole," said Dave. "We should hire him."

I was a happy boy. I didn't know it at the time, but I was about to start my dream job.

Firing an Asshole Client

AGENCIES GET FIRED ALL the time. I remember learning early on that the day you win an account is one day closer to the day you eventually lose that same piece of business.

Rarely does the agency fire the client. But we did one glorious day at DDB.

I was the account supervisor for an online dating resource called Kiss.com. It preceded Match.com and many others in the early days of finding love online.

Our client was pretty old school, and it pissed me off. His management strategy was to suck up to me (for no apparent reason), while belittling my hard-working account team behind my back. We were doing some great work, but it was obvious early on that we would never make him happy.

His favorite routine would be to wait until 4:30 p.m. on Friday afternoons and call me with a list of complaints about how lazy and incompetent my DDB team had been over the previous week. If I wasn't around, he would rant on voicemail. Every single week.

This was getting old quickly. It was his way to ruin an otherwise great week and the upcoming weekend.

After a few weeks of this crap, I finally turned to Tom Phillips, who ran our PR division at the agency. I explained the dilemma, playing some of the voice mails I had saved for evidence.

Tom was angry, but not at our team. "We need to fire these clowns," said Tom. "We're not making enough from Kiss to put up with this shit."

I smiled at this point. "I'll go talk to Elgin," he said.

Ron agreed. "Let's fire their ass," he told Tom.

I was never prouder to work at DDB. You mean the welfare of our team was more important than profit?

Hell yes. I gathered our team to pass on the news. You would have thought we won the Lottery. Lots of hugging and high fives. In addition to a client who couldn't figure out why we booted them off our roster.

Well done, DDB.

What Agencies Will Do to Win Business

I'VE ALWAYS LOVED THE thrill of the new business pitch. My agency bosses have always hated the concept.

It's easy to see why. If an agency makes it to the finals for a national account, they will have invested tons of money and time in the hopes of winning a piece of business. The presentations usually become a big dog and pony show—which of course, inspired the cover of this book.

I've been involved in hundreds of pitches over the years: from one-on-one client presentations to mega agency theater. A video was once produced of me on a farm milking a cow for Elgin Syferd's bid for the Dairy Farmers of Washington account. Classic agency magic under the supervision of our leader, Jan Edmondson. We didn't win—and I haven't touched a cow's udder since. Not even once. Really.

At WONGDOODY, I developed a full program of community events to make the idea of outrageous lending fees for payday loans from Moneytree seem like a fine idea. Nope, it wasn't. Didn't win. And thank God, I've never been that desperate for cash.

For Beck's Beer, I created a year-long series of promos throughout the Puget Sound area designed to encourage people to drink a lot of overpriced imported beer. The key program was Beck's & Decks, held Wednesday through Friday in the summer months on some of Seattle's best outdoor restaurant decks. I had a vast amount of background in the category because I used to drink a lot of beer on restaurant decks. We won that business.

But the one that still makes me laugh was the ES national pitch for Nutrisystem, the weight loss company.

Ron and Dave always preached marketing integration, so we prepared for the finals with a tremendous presentation of advertising, public relations and promotions. When the rather large head of marketing arrived for the pitch, I kept thinking: does this clown even use his own product? Hmmm.

We had a conference room that had a camera in one corner that could send a feed of the proceedings to another room. I had to be on my game because I knew my bosses would be watching.

There were about a dozen of us from the agency in the presentation. As usual, we spent the first 20 minutes laying out our communications and sales strategy. It's usually very important for clients to see how we think, and how we intend to solve their marketing problems.

The client sat at the head of the table. He was sweating—a lot—and seemed very disinterested in all the well thought out strategy.

Right in the middle of the presentation, he waves his hands and says "Stop…stop."

I was mentally on cruise control because I wasn't scheduled to present for another hour. Or so I thought.

"This is all good, but where are the promotions?" he barked. "I want to see promotions."

Everyone's eyes fell on me. "That would be Scott," said our leader. "Scott…can you present the promos now?"

Dave Syferd later told me that they were laughing in the other room, watching me pee my pants at the sudden change in direction. It was showtime, whether I was ready or not. And I wasn't.

I stood up and walked the fat, sweaty client through a series of consumer promotions. As I remember, I presented the promos at warp speed.

He just kept nodding. And sweating.

When I was done, we still hadn't presented the bulk of our ideas including the ad campaign…but he was done. He got up, thanked us and made his way out the door with our presentation materials.

As the room emptied, I just sat there. Dave walked in, sat down and gave me a pat on the back. "Janbo…that all sort of sucked," he said.

"Ya think?" I countered.

"I'm not sure we want to work with those guys anyway," he said.

You can guess the ending. We didn't win. But in a way, we did, not having to work with a dork for a client. And a sweaty one at that.

One Argument in 30 Years

DAVE SYFERD WAS MY hero, mentor, and wonderful friend. He was also my boss at Elgin Syferd, and in 30+ years of knowing each other, he only wanted to fire my ass once. This is that story.

One of my best friends in the world—Barry Bartlett—was getting married. I volunteered to throw the bachelor party. It was going to be a small, undignified event with a party bus, steaks, cigars, and strip clubs.

My friend provided a guest list, and I recognized every name but one.

After reviewing the degenerates on the list, I realized a disgusting invite was needed. And I don't mean local market disgusting—this called for world class disgusting.

I won't go into detail about what I wrote, previewing the night's activities for the attendees…but it was bad. Really bad. In my 30-year-old head, the party needed this kind of invite.

I wanted it to look nice, too. So, like an idiot, I printed the invite out on Elgin Syferd letterhead and mailed them in Elgin Syferd envelopes.

To make matters worse, I ran them through our company postage meter.

Danger, Will Robinson—danger!

I received RSVPs from everyone on the list—except from the one name I didn't recognize.

A couple of days later, Dave called me into his office. He was not happy. I had never seen that face before.

He was standing at his desk, holding a copy of one of the invites.

"Janbo...are you responsible for this piece of trash?" he asked.

Hmmm...my first thought was to deny any involvement. And run like hell.

I swallowed hard. "Uh...yeah," I said. I was busted.

"I received this from one of our clients today, wondering what kind of idiot writes this crap and sends it out on our company letterhead," he said. "Are you freaking insane, Janbo?"

The answer, of course, was yes. My response was even more insane.

"Dave, I totally get it," I said. "I'll pay for the letterhead, envelopes and postage—that's my bad," I said.

He got even madder.

"Look, you dumb shit," he said. "It's not about the materials. By issuing this on our letterhead, your content is a reflection of our agency. What the hell were you thinking?"

By now, I'm trembling. My eyes began to fill with tears.

"Janbo...this invite is truly disgusting," he continued. "I'm not against this party—hell, where was my invite? But this was a knucklehead move by a guy who should know better. I'm very disappointed in you."

A shot to my heart from my boss and mentor.

"I should fire your ass today...but I'm not going to," he said. "Just learn from this, OK?"

I went back to my office and cried some more.

When my buddy learned what happened, we scaled down the bachelor party. As I remember, it was a pretty tame affair.

Over the years, I shared many glasses of wine with Dave. If he wanted to bring me down to size, he'd bring up the invite fiasco, smiling as I'd squirm.

Just before he passed away, Dave and I were at Sport Restaurant, and he brought it up again. "Jesus, Dave, after 30 years…let it go," I said.

"Never, Janbo," he smiled. "Never."

Who Wants Some Chili?

NALLEY'S FINE FOODS IN Tacoma was a client I first worked on at Cole & Weber in 1983, and then followed me to three other agencies. I guess they liked my promotional programs for their potato chips, pickles, chili, stew, and salad dressings.

One campaign stands out. Nalley's wanted to reach consumers in the Midwest to show that by adding simple fresh ingredients to their "canned meat" (chili/stew) offerings, you could produce (in their words) a "hearty Midwest meal."

Seriously.

I came up with the idea of producing a cookbook featuring Seattle-based food expert Karen Gregorakis, available free from Nalley's. We'd book Karen into TV and radio talk show appearances in lovely places like Omaha, Nebraska in the middle of winter. Yes, PR can be glamorous at times.

To prepare for the tour, I asked Karen how much chili and stew I should order from Nalley's for her cooking demos. She felt that 40 cans of chili and 40 cans of stew would do the trick.

A few days later, I looked out my apartment window in West Seattle. There was a huge Nalley's rig idling out on the street.

"Are you Scott Janzen?" the driver asked. "I've got your chili and stew right here." I expected a couple of cases of both.

He started to unload 40 cases of chili and 40 cases of stew. Holy shit, I thought—I'm screwed.

I frantically tried to explain the error. The driver smiled but shook his head. Apparently, he did not want to haul it all back to Nalley Valley in Tacoma.

"You like our chili and stew?" he asked. "Uh, yeah," was my intelligent reply. "Well, let's just load this into your apartment and we'll call it good," he said.

How much room could 80 cases take? The bounty filled my living room, bedroom, kitchen, and closets. I signed his receipt and said goodbye.

I started making phone calls.

"You want a case of chili? How about stew?" I asked to friends and co-workers. Suddenly, I was very popular. None of us had any money, so free chili and stew was the perfect holiday gift. I even offered it to ladies at the end of dates with a goodnight kiss.

I dined on Nalley's chili and stew for three years. Not exactly a culinary memory.

The Birth of J&A

AT SOME POINT, EVERY PR pro wants to start their own practice. Most of the time, it's not a great idea.

I dreamed of opening my own shop. I'd call it Janzen & Associates. I was Janzen and my mostly imaginary "associates" would be my staff.

In 1990 I was working as a VP/PR at Borders Perrin Norrander, a Portland-based advertising agency with a Seattle office. We had amazing accounts including Kenworth and Washington's Lottery, led by Pete Hatt, a terrific CEO and leader. It's the agency I met Larry Asher, one of the best creative directors I've ever worked with.

We were mostly an ad shop. My VP partner in crime, Doug Siefkes, specialized in B2B accounts—especially those in the trucking industry—and I did the consumer stuff like the Lottery and others.

BPN offered PR because many of our clients asked for it. But most of our revenue came from advertising. Doug and I knew that BPN wanted out of the PR business, so we hatched an idea and marched into Pete's office.

"Pete, is it safe to say you don't really understand PR and would eventually like to get out of the business?" we asked.

Pete slyly smiled at his desk. "What's your point?" he said.

Knowing we were about to drop a bomb, I cleared my throat and offered: "What if Doug and I took our PR accounts—not touching any of your ad revenues—and started our own PR shops? We'd work closely with BPN but wouldn't be employees. Whatcha think?"

I think I stopped breathing for a few moments. Pete looked at the two of us and thought that might be a fine idea.

Doug and I walked out to First Avenue in front of the agency, high-fiving each other and stunned at what had just happened.

My buddy opened what would eventually become SiefkesPetit Communications in Issaquah, still in business after 30 years. I'm not surprised. Doug knows his shit.

I opened the first incarnation of Janzen & Associates in 1991, with the Lottery as my cornerstone account. My offices were in a shared space building across the street from the Kingdome.

As I proudly attached my J&A logo to the office door, I remember some wise counsel delivered to be by Marc DeLaunay, my boss at Elgin Syferd.

"The excitement of seeing your logo on a business card or front door will go away quickly when the invoice and other start-up costs are due," he said. Yep.

On my first day I called my Lottery client, who had promised to transfer their $5,000/month retainer account to J&A. They told me it was going to happen—but not for six months.

Oh boy. I had just signed a year's lease on the space. I had a cool new office and no clients. So, I started to hustle and made a lot of calls. I picked up some project work and a cool company in Olympia called Pacific Communications (PACCOM), who provided marketing and advertising production to smaller retail clients. Jim Jenner, president, saved my butt for those first six months until the Lottery and other accounts kicked in. Thank you, Jim.

J&A would eventually move to offices in Pioneer Square and Bellevue. One time Evelyn Yenson, Lottery director, came to see my Pioneer Square offices. She climbed a lot of stairs to reach my third floor space. "We're not paying you enough, are we?" she asked. I just smiled.

My first employee was Laura Kingman, who devised a compelling argument for me to hire her. She was cheap. But Laura did solid work and has gone on to great acclaim with the Washington State Department of Transportation. My last employee was Heather Knox, a writer and communications pro who joined my firm in Bellevue and has since held management positions with Amazon, Microsoft and many others. I am so proud of both.

I was packing moving boxes on my final day of business when I got a call from Jay Rockey, legendary PR pro and owner of The Rockey Company. I had never met Jay, so I was surprised by the call.

"Scott, I've heard a rumor that you're closing your doors," he said. "I'm wondering if you might be interested in selling your firm to us?"

"Uh, Jay...there's nothing left to sell," I said. "All of my accounts have been transitioned to the freelancers I worked with—so the only thing left to acquire is me."

His response was swift.

"Oh, well thank you, Scott," said Jay. "Good luck in your future endeavors." Click.

I started to laugh and finished packing. Timing is everything.

My Kingdom for a Bobblehead

I LOVE BOBBLEHEADS. MY earliest memory is owning a generic Seattle Pilots bobblehead as a kid. Alas, gone forever.

At DDB, I supervised the Woodinville-based BDA business. The nation's largest merchandise agency is involved in lots of different things covering the business and sports worlds—including bobbleheads. Lucky for me. Sort of.

Our client was a former Elgin Syferd employee, Steve Avanessian, who was always looking to get the word out about specialty created bobbleheads for MLB teams.

My office at DDB was filled with more than 250 bobbleheads. Most of them were MLB players (I had lots of Ichiro bobbles) but I also had wrestlers from the WWF, Fidel Castro and Jesus Christ. Most of these were from BDA, while others came to me as gifts.

My associate on the account was the talented and resourceful Heidi Happonen, who somehow always found a story angle for the latest MLB team's bobblehead. Many times, she wandered into my office with the look of a woman who was tired of trying to make media magic happen with yet another bobblehead.

More often than not, she found a sports reporter who would give a crap about the latest giveaway. Thank you, Heidi, for always delivering the press coverage.

My office was an agency tour stop, whether I was conducting business or not. The father of a co-worker, Sarabeth Anderson, built me special shelving to display my bounty. I wanted to start charging admission.

When I was leaving DDB in 2005, I packed up a lot of stuff, including 20 of my favorite bobbleheads. But I didn't want to move the other 200+, so I sent out a sent out a company-wide email that simply said: Free bobbleheads. Stop by Scott Janzen's office.

For the next few hours, I welcomed co-workers I had never seen or met before, all wanting free bobbleheads. They gobbled up everything—including Castro.

Today, I have one bobblehead left: The San Diego Chicken. Actually, make that two. I had one made up of me kicking a soccer ball. Like most bobbleheads, it looks nothing like me, except it has better hair and soccer skills.

Life at Trupanion

I WENT TO WORK for Trupanion in 2016. It's one of the few non-agency jobs I've held in my career.

Trupanion provides medical insurance for cats and dogs, and I was their director of communications. I loved my job. During my nearly three years there, we insured more than 500,000 pets in North America. My amazing comm team, including Michael Nank (PR Manager), Tara Sharp (Social Media Manager) and Marissa Villegas (Content Manager) made me look good on a daily basis. Matter of fact, the first thing I did when I was hired was to fire our PR/social agency—that's how great my internal team was. We were consistently number one in media coverage and social media exposure among our competitors. Kind of cool.

So many wonderful memories. In no particular order:

When I took a horrific fall in my apartment, breaking my left ankle in three places, my Trupanion team rallied to my aid. In addition, wonderful co-workers like Nicole Thomson (Senior Visual Designer) fed me chili and kept my spirits up.

After the surgeries, I was transferred to a rehab center from hell on Queen Anne. I realized everyone knew about my injury but our CEO, Darryl Rawlings. On a quiet Sunday morning, I sent him an email with an update. A few hours later, he showed up in my room. Darryl took one look around and said "This isn't going to do. I've got some ideas. I'll be back in a few hours."

He returned late Sunday afternoon and converted my room into a working office, with noise-cancelling headphones, power strips and lots of other stuff, including dinner from Dick's. He tossed it to me and said, "You need real food." As I scarfed down the burger, fries and shake, I just smiled watching Darryl convert my room into an office.

Between medical insurance and checks the company wrote on my behalf, Trupanion covered more than $200,000 in medical expenses. I will forever be grateful. All for a broken ankle? There's more to the story. Keep reading—more details coming up.

When I returned to the Trupanion corporate office, I was navigating its racetrack oval in a wheelchair. Because I couldn't walk, I wondered what would happen in an emergency. We were on the fifth floor and elevators would shut down in a fire.

It didn't take long to find out. The fire alarm went off one morning. Oh shit, I thought. I'm going to die at work. This will suck.

Margi Tooth, our CMO at the time, came running out of a meeting. "Somebody help Scott!" she said. Sounds like a good idea, but what the hell does that mean?

Richard Wang, a big strong dude in our digital group, picked me up out of the wheelchair, and proceeded to carry me down five flights of stairs to the ground floor.

It felt like the scene from *An Officer and a Gentlemen*, except I was larger than Debra Winger and we weren't in love.

What if Richard drops me, I thought. What if I burn up and die was my other thought. I decided to hold on for dear life and take my chances.

I was deposited back into my wheelchair when we hit the ground floor. The fire wasn't much, but it scared the hell out of everyone.

Yes, we produced great campaigns and memorable programs during my time there. But when I think about Trupanion, I'll remember the co-workers who became wonderful friends, like Colleen O'Leary and Ian Parker. And the 150+ dogs (and a few brave cats) in our office on a daily basis who were always at my side for a face rub or treat.

Nice Scooter, Janbo

IT ALL STARTED AS a simple question from my doctor during my annual physical about six years ago.

"All of your numbers look good, Scott," he said. "Anything else going on with you?"

"Well, it's probably just because I'm getting older," I told him, "but it's getting harder for me to get out of my car or office chair. But no big deal."

"Humor me on this one," he said, with the stern face only a doctor can provide. "Let's run some tests."

No problem, I thought. Sure, let's run a few tests. Nearly 20 tests later over two months and they still couldn't figure it out. Then, I started to fall occasionally. It didn't make any sense. I was soon checked by a specialist in muscle diseases at the University of Washington. They ordered a biopsy.

"You've got Inclusion Body Myositis (IBM)," I was told. IBM is a rare inflammatory muscle disease that hits older adults. It hit me in my legs and hands, making it difficult to walk up a flight of stairs or, frankly, to go from point A to point B. It's a progressive disease that slowly weakens your body—and there is no cure. Rock legend Peter Frampton was diagnosed with this a couple of years ago after falling often on stage.

I did not take the news well.

I'll just learn to live with it, I thought. And I did for a short time, keeping my secret mostly to myself.

One night, I took a horrific fall in my back bedroom and was rushed to the ER. I broke my left ankle in three places. I told the ER doctor that I was trying to land a triple axel—he didn't find that funny.

I had surgery and they fixed the ankle. But I was off my feet for months as IBM did its thing. I started with physical therapy at home but took three more falls. My main doctor at Swedish ordered me to make the wheelchair my friend and not try to walk unless I was being supervised.

Ugh.

Here's some good news. I found a wonderful physical therapy center at Lake Union called Movement Systems—ironically occupying the former home of Triples and Kayak, two favorite watering holes of mine from the 1990s. Karma, yes?

My team is now led by the wonderful Laura Broudy, who took the reins from Nate Hadley and Emma Mitsui when they left Movement Systems. They all have worked me hard and we're making progress, with a big goal: I will walk again.

Let me repeat: I WILL WALK AGAIN. Not sure how long it will take, but it's going to happen.

This is the first time I'm openly talking about my IBM because I don't want anyone's pity. Big gifts and large sums of money? Sure. But don't feel sorry for me. Just cheer when you eventually see me walking towards you.

In April 2021, I was nearly killed on my scooter when a recycling truck driver took a free right turn and took out the front axle of my ride. I turned away from the impact, and my reflexes saved my life. The guy didn't stop and drove down Second Avenue. Lucky for me, I had lots of witnesses who got me to safety.

As I sat on my mangled scooter, waiting for Yellow Cab to rescue me and somehow get home, I shook my head. And then I smiled. Like George Bailey, I've had a wonderful life. My girl Kelly Clarkson sings: What doesn't kill you makes you stronger.

And who doesn't want to see me on the dance floor again?

My All-Time Favorite Clients

I DEVELOPED A SPECIALTY for retail and travel throughout my agency career from the more than 300 accounts I've managed.

What makes a great client? No, it's not the ones that spend the most moola—although that's a wonderful trait in a client. Trust me. But I love clients who understand that great marketing comes from a collaborative effort between the agency and client.

Here's a top ten list of my all-time favorite clients—in no particular order:

Holland America Line: I've worked on this biz from the mid-1980s to today. Erik Elvejord, director of PR, is as solid as they come, from day-to-day media relations to crisis communications.

SuperMall of the Great Northwest: The Auburn mall has become an outlet center, but I have wonderful memories of the work we did and Lynn Beck, marketing director. I met Lynn when she did an informational interview with me years earlier. When she smiled at me during our pitch at Fearey, I knew we had won the account.

Nalley's Fine Foods: I started working on the account at C&W, and they followed me to three other agencies. I learned way too much about pickles, salad dressing, chili, stew, and other products. If you've never tasted a hot potato chip bouncing on the conveyor line, you haven't lived.

Washington's Lottery: I worked with a great team, starting with Evelyn Yenson, Lottery director. They trusted my big ideas—and it seemed to always pay off. Evelyn asked me one time why I wasn't buying tickets for a big Lotto jackpot. "Because legally, I can't win," I said. "That's not a good reason," she answered.

YMCA of Greater Seattle: Again, I worked with a terrific team who always listened to the outside counsel we provided. I'm especially proud of the "Stand Up for Kids" capital campaign that raised millions for local YMCA improvements.

Beck's Beer: The account opened the door for me to work on several brands over the years. We had the opportunity to do some exceptional work for Beck's, both at restaurants and grocery stores. And we sold a lot of beer.

Massage Envy: I had never enjoyed the pleasure of a massage until I started working on their business. After my first massage I thought...this is pretty cool. I need to spread the word.

McDonald's of Western Washington: I learned more about marketing from my years on this business than any other account. Love or hate their food (and I love me a McRib!), they know how to market their products.

Seattle Renaissance: A wonderful hotel that provided me with the opportunity to do international work for the brand and see the world. I will always be grateful.

BDA: The nation's leading merchandise company, with a client that was formerly my co-worker at Elgin Syferd. Hated the drive to Woodinville but loved the work and results we got.

I'll Always Be a Patches Pal

PRO BONO IS A Latin phrase for professional work done voluntarily and without payment. I've had many traditional paying clients try to stiff me over the years, but I'm not talking about *that* kind of pro bono.

Work I've undertaken for area non-profit clients has been some of the most meaningful work I've ever done. The YMCA of Greater Seattle is a terrific example. I was first asked to serve on a communications committee in the 1990s with other Seattle PR pros, under the direction of their terrific director of communications Monica Elenbaas. Over the next 20+ years, it evolved from pro bono to paid (Fearey Group) back to pro bono to serving on the Board of Directors for the organization to paid again (Janzen & Associates).

I believe in their mission. Always have and always will. Overall, I've done work for more than a dozen non-profit organizations.

Sometimes, you take on a pro bono mission for personal reasons. I grew up in Seattle as a huge fan of J.P. Patches, Seattle's favorite clown until his death in 2012. He ruled local television on KIRO TV from 1958-81. I watched him in the morning before school, when I got home from school and on Saturday mornings. When the show ended, it was regarded as one of the longest running locally produced children's shows in the U.S. Even after the show left the air, J.P. still made lots of personal appearances throughout the area for Boomers like me.

I was a Patches Pal. And I'm still a Patches Pal, all these years later.

In the early 2000s, I had the opportunity to bid on a once-in-a-lifetime experience with J.P.: brunch for ten at the Space Needle with my favorite clown. I won the silent charity auction for $500—what a bargain!

I didn't realize that J.P. could only sip coffee when he's in full make-up, and I apologized to my hero several times. But I made sure that J.P. was sitting across from me over the next 90 minutes. I had so many questions to ask him. He was funny, polite, and told the ten of us so many terrific stories of his television life.

At one point, I blurted out: "J.P., you'll always be a rock star to me."

"Like Eddie Vedder?" he asked. My God...J.P. knows Pearl Jam. "Better!" I said. He just smiled.

In 2008, I was asked by Bryan Johnston, author of a wonderful book on J.P. and local creative pro if I could provide pro bono PR assistance to help raise money to build a bronze statue of J.P. and his on-screen "girlfriend", Gertrude (Bob Newman), in Seattle's Fremont neighborhood. Of course, I said yes.

One night our group gathered to see some early design work from the sculptor. I knew everyone in the car except for one gentleman in the back seat. "I thought you guys had already met," said Bryan. "Scott, meet Chris Wedes."

My hero without his makeup. I froze for a moment, because I never wanted to see J.P. when he wasn't J.P. Chris smiled and shook my hand. I almost wept.

"Thanks for being a part of all this," he said. I told him of our brunch years earlier at the Space Needle. He said he remembered, but he probably didn't—who cares. All I wanted to do was to get that statue built. Our team raised more than $150,000 for the statue, and you can see it today in all its glory.

The joy of J.P. Patches at the dedication, with hundreds of fans professing their love for our favorite clown, was a memory I'll never forget.

Lots of Seattle Agencies

WHEN I TALK ABOUT my agency career, I always tell people I worked at a lot of Seattle shops. Only a few still exist today, which means I'm really old or…I'm really old.

I learned something from all my colleagues at these different shops. A few were full-service agencies, offering advertising, public relations, digital, media and design. Others were PR-only shops. Some random thoughts, in no particular order, about some favorites from my agency career. And apologies in advance for all the names.

Elgin Syferd: Loved this place, led by two industry giants, Ron Elgin and Dave Syferd. They believed that advertising and public relations should have an equal seat at the big kid's table, so Elgin (advertising) and Syferd (PR) built a shop with professionals who were experts in their respective fields but understood how the disciplines can and should work together. I spent six years at ES, working with terrific pros like Sydney Hunsdale, Jan Edmondson, Pete DeLaunay, Marc DeLaunay, Tom Phillips, Katie Bender, April Graves, Nancy Howell, Tim Pavish, Karen Patricelli, Barb Edmondson, Tom O'Rourke, Kevin Burrus, Kevin Nolan, Jane Shanklin, Laurie McLennan, Nancy Monsarrat, Bob Frause, and so many others. When I left, I was the fifth longest in seniority at the shop. Now, I'm just senior.

DDB Seattle: Elgin Syferd was purchased by DDB, a global agency, so it was an easy decision for me to "come home" to the agency, in which I spent another five years from 2000-2005. So many of my pals were still there, but

I met people like Dan McConnell, Gaby Adam, April Matson, Michelle Lo, Scott Battishill, Michelle Stevens, Leslie Shattuck, Janice Merlino, Arlene Fairfield, Alex Barth, Teri Bauer, Chris Lloyd, Fred Hammerquist, Heidi Happonen, Doreen Jarman, Stephanie Pearson, George Nguyen, Hillary Miller, Chris Lloyd, Eric Gutierrez, and Eric Walter.

WONGDOODY: Primarily an ad agency, but I was brought on to try and build a PR team in Seattle and Los Angeles. Led by Tracy Wong and Pat Doody. Was only there for a couple of years, but I got to work with Jennifer Cody and Connie Sung Moyle who did brilliant PR for our LA clients, and most importantly, introduced this dinosaur to the concept of social media. I will forever be grateful.

The Fearey Group: Loved this agency. It started with the brilliance of Pat Fearey, but we hired so many cool professionals who are mentioned elsewhere in these pages. I remember when we had one computer with access to the "World Wide Web," and we all clamored to use it before we all were online. I was a hero to the staff when I helped introduce the concept of Casual Friday to an agency in which we wore suits every single day.

Sharp Hartwig: Led by Dave Sharp and Cynthia Hartwig. I was only there six months because the agency chose to cease operations right after I joined as a VP. That sucked. But they did wonderful, strategic work and I eventually hired Dave's daughter, Tara, to work with me at Trupanion. It's a small world after all.

Borders Perrin Norrander: It was BP&N when I worked there, and we were in Portland and Seattle. Now, just Portland. I will forever be grateful to Pete Hatt, our CEO, for hiring me and then letting me go start the first incarnation of Janzen & Associates in 1991. Led by Stephanie Ager, I got to work with professionals like Doug Siefkes, Marcia Rhodes, and Mike Wasem, who all went on to amazing careers.

Cole & Weber: Once a powerhouse ad/PR shop. I got to work with Jim McFarland, Michael Quick and Rick Bechtel, among others. When I left the agency and Nalley's Fine Foods followed me to Elgin Syferd, the head of the PR division tried to sue me, saying an idea I created at C&W was their idea. First, I created the program at ES—so bite me. And don't try to also sue Elgin Syferd at the same time. "Don't worry about it," said Elgin. "We're going to go after the little f**ker, " referring to the diminutive PR director. Potential lawsuit was gone in hours. They blinked.

What I've Learned

ESQUIRE PUBLISHES "WHAT I'VE Learned," an interesting series of musings from famous people on life lessons. I'm never going to be asked what *I've* learned, so to close this book…well, here's some thoughts:

- Treasure your friends, and they'll always have your back.

- PR is often common sense at $200 an hour.

- If your client asks you to lie and mislead the media, just say no.

- If a cute hostess sits on your lap in a Bangkok bar, just say no.

- Most of your PR heroes will die before their time. But their wisdom stays with you forever.

- A turkey sandwich from Bakeman's in Downtown Seattle was my favorite lunch. But the conversations were even better.

- Never eat at your desk on a regular basis. Nobody is impressed.

- Likewise, get your work done in 40 hours and then leave the shop. Do what brings you joy.

- Always play the role of mentor if asked and provide the same quality of guidance you received from your mentors.

- PR awards are, for the most part, worthless. And I've won my share.

- Unless you're announcing the second coming, avoid staging press conferences at all costs.

- Job titles are important early in your career. As you get older, you realize it's all self-serving BS.

- A great marriage is hard work. Cris, I wish I had worked harder. You deserved better from me. I'm sorry.

- Think long and hard before you press "send" on emails. They will often come back and bite you on the ass. Especially if you press "reply to all" instead of "reply."

- Always thank your team and share praise for a job well done.

- If you work for me, give me your best for eight hours. Then leave our office on time, and go do what makes you happy.

- Stay away from assholes, in work and your personal life. They're toxic.

- If you must fire someone, tear off the bandage quickly. Deliver the message, tell them thank-you for their contributions and let them have their dignity.

- Life is too short to work with shitty clients. If one is making your team's life hell, fire their ass.

- Laugh a lot. For no apparent reason.

- I was told at an early age that "life is not a dress rehearsal." I disagree. My second act is going to kick ass.

- Work hard. But play even harder.

Thank You!

A VERY SPECIAL THANK YOU to those who contributed to my GoFundMe campaign to make this book happen. I hope I haven't forgotten any of my generous friends who believed in this project...and me. You're the best.

Ann Marie Ricard

David Sharp

David Fishman

Mary Linn

John McMullen

Theresa Arbow-O'Connor

Greg Carter

Julian Rivera

Teri Bauer

Ian Parker

Chris Settle

Terry Polyak

Katie Sims

Tom Phillips

Susan Belanich

Dawn Zimmerman

Rita Giese

Colleen O'Leary

Lorena Stookey

John Hollett

Stephanie Pearson

Michele Stevens

Rita Bjork

Jackie Hennessey

Kyle Vixie

Shevaun Brown

Dane Estes

Jennifer Cody

Heidi Happonen

Steve Lawson

Laura McLeod

Diana Ferrier

Sandra & Ed Hiersche

Michael Saunderson

Tammy Fuqua

Kim Fuqua

Susan & Michael VanTrojen

Patti Parrish

Ron Elgin

Jerry May

Bob Smith

Larry Asher

Jan Edmondson